Guidelines on the Use of Tiered Environmental Impact Statements for Transportation Projects

Requested by:

American Association of State Highway and Transportation Officials (AASHTO)
Standing Committee on the Environment

Prepared by:

PB Americas, Inc. and Perkins Coie LLP

June 2009

The information contained in this report was prepared as part of NCHRP Project 25-25, Task 38 National Cooperative Highway Research Program, Transportation Research Board.

Acknowledgments

This study was requested by the American Association of State Highway and Transportation Officials (AASHTO), and conducted as part of the National Cooperative Highway Research Program (NCHRP) Project 25-25. The NCHRP is supported by annual voluntary contributions from state Departments of Transportation. Project 25-25 provides funding for quick response studies on behalf of the AASHTO Standing Committee on the Environment. The report was prepared by Ann Koby of PB Americas, Inc. (PB) as the Principal Investigator. William Malley and Joanna Thies of Perkins Coie, and Jason Miles of PB, were all research investigators. Cynthia Burbank of PB was the Research Advisor. Christopher Hedges, NCHRP Senior Program Officer, was the project manager. The work was guided by a task group chaired by Dr. Gail Anne D'Avino, and included Maryann Blouin, Doug Booher, Mark S. Kross, Michael Murdoch, and Barney O'Quinn.

Disclaimer

The opinions and conclusions expressed or implied are those of the research agency that performed the research and are not necessarily those of the Transportation Research Board, the American Association of State Highway and Transportation Officials, or its sponsors. The information contained in this document was taken directly from the submission of the authors. This document is not a report of the Transportation Research Board or of the National Research Council.

Reference herein to any specific commercial product, process, or service by trade name, trademark, manufacturer, or otherwise does not necessarily constitute or imply its endorsement, recommendation, or favoring by NCHRP, the Transportation Research Board or the National Research Council.

Table of Contents

Appendices

1 <u>List of Acronyms</u>

AASHTO	American Association of State Highway and Transportation Officials
CE	Categorical Exclusion
CEQ	Council on Environmental Quality
CWA	Clean Water Act
CFR	Code of Federal Regulations
DEIS	Draft Environmental Impact Statement
DOT	Department of Transportation
EA	Environmental Assessment
EIS	Environmental Impact Statement
EPA	United States Environmental Protection Agency
ESA	Endangered Species Act
FEIS	Final Environmental Impact Statement
FHWA	Federal Highway Administration
FRA	Federal Rail Administration
FTA	Federal Transit Administration
GIS	Geographic Information System
INDOT	Indiana Department of Transportation
LEDPA	Least Environmentally Damaging Practicable Alternative
MOA	Memorandum of Agreement
MOU	Memorandum of Understanding
MPO	Metropolitan Planning Organization
NCHRP	National Cooperative Highway Research Program
NEPA	National Environmental Policy Act
NHPA	National Historic Preservation Act
NOI	Notice of Intent
ROD	Record of Decision
ROW	Right of Way
SAFETEA-LU	Safe, Accountable, Flexible, Efficient Transportation Equity Act: A Legacy for Users
SEIS	Supplemental Environmental Impact Statement
USC	United States Code
USDOT	United States Department of Transportation

2 <u>Introduction</u>

This report provides guidelines on the use of tiering to complete the National Environmental Policy Act (NEPA) process for surface transportation projects that require approval by the Federal Highway Administration (FHWA), Federal Transit Administration (FTA), or Federal Railroad Administration (FRA). The report is based on a review of over 20 tiered NEPA studies that have been initiated between 1999 and September 2008 for highway, transit, and passenger rail projects and is accompanied by a technical memorandum that describes the research methodology, and documents key factors associated with the success of tiered studies while identifying the greatest challenges tiered studies faced.

This report consists of three substantive parts.

- **Section 3   Tiered EISs – What You Need to Know** provides basic background information on tiering, including a discussion of relevant regulations, guidance, and case law on tiering under NEPA. It also briefly discusses the pros and cons of tiering.

- **Section 4   State of the Practice and Managing Risk** summarizes recent experiences with tiering for surface transportation projects (highways, transit, and passenger rail). It includes an overview of studies in which a tiered approach has been used. It also discusses key factors associated with success in tiered studies, and discusses potential strategies for anticipating and managing tiering-related risks.

- **Section 5   Checklist of Issues to Consider** provides an annotated checklist of issues to consider in deciding whether to use tiering and in deciding how to carry out a tiered study.

Appendices A through D include excerpts of relevant regulations and guidance related to tiering. Appendix E contains a table with basic descriptions of tiered studies initiated for surface transportation projects since 1999. The technical memorandum is included in Appendix F, describing the research methodology and documenting the key factors associated with a successful project and summarizing challenges projects using a tiered process have encountered. Appendix G provides a brief project description of the projects used for this research.

3 Tiered EISs – What You Need to Know

3.1 Basics of Tiering

The basic concept of tiering is straightforward. Rather than preparing a single environmental impact statement (EIS) as the basis for approving the entire project, the agency conducts two or more rounds – or "tiers" – of environmental review. In Tier 1, the agency typically prepares an EIS that analyzes a program or large project on a broad scale. In Tier 2, the agency prepares one or more additional NEPA documents, which examine individual projects or sections in greater detail.

The challenge in preparing a tiered study is determining the details of the tiered approach. The agencies preparing a tiered study must make several important decisions, such as:

- What decisions will be made in each tier?

- How much detail is appropriate in each tier?

- How will non-NEPA requirements – e.g., Section 4(f), historic preservation consultation, endangered species consultation, and wetlands permitting – be addressed at each tier?

- How will agencies and the public be involved in the tiered process?

- What will be done to educate agencies and the public about the tiered process?

The answers to these questions vary from project to project. An approach that works well for one project may be a poor fit for another. The annotated checklist in Section 5 is intended to assist lead agencies and project sponsors in answering these questions.

Tiering is typically adopted for three main reasons: (1) complexity of managing the NEPA process for lengthy corridors; (2) desire to authorize corridor preservation, where construction is not anticipated for many years; and (3) lack of funding to complete a traditional EIS which require more detailed studies than is typically required for a Tier 1 EIS. Another reason for tiering, which usually coincides with a lack of funding, is to prevent the numerous studies associated with a traditional EIS from becoming outdated because the funding shortage prevents the project from moving forward.

3.2 Legal Framework for Tiering

The concept of tiering is defined in the NEPA regulations issued by the Council on Environmental Quality (CEQ), and is further explained in FHWA and FTA's joint regulations for implementing NEPA and Section 4(f). The CEQ and FHWA/FTA also have issued guidance documents that address tiering, the most significant of which is a memorandum issued by FHWA in 2001 for the I-70 project in Missouri. The regulations and guidance provide overall direction, but also allow flexibility in determining how to prepare a tiered environmental study. Key provisions from the regulations and guidance are summarized below.

3.2.1 CEQ Regulations

The CEQ regulations recognize the use of tiering as one option for complying with NEPA. The CEQ regulations address tiering in two places: Section 1502.20 and Section 1508.38. For the full text of these provisions, refer to Appendix A.

Section 1502.20. Section 1502.20 states that federal agencies "are encouraged to tier their environmental impact statements to eliminate repetitive discussions of the same issues and to focus on the actual issues ripe for decision at each level of environmental review." Other key points include:

- The Tier 1 study should be an EIS. The Tier 2 study can be an EIS, an Environmental Assessment (EA), or a combination of different classes of action. (FHWA has determined that a Categorical Exclusion (CE) determination also may be prepared at the Tier 2 stage, if the CE criteria are met.)[1]

- The Tier 2 study should summarize the broader issues discussed in the Tier 1 study and incorporate those discussions by reference. The Tier 2 study should focus on the issues specific to the Tier 2 action.

- The Tier 2 study should state how individuals can access the Tier 1 document.

Section 1508.28. Section 1508.28 is the Definitions section of the CEQ regulations. Defines tiering as "the coverage of general matters in broader environmental impact statements (such as national program or policy statements) with subsequent narrower statements or environmental analyses (such as regional or basin-wide program statements or ultimately site-specific statements) incorporating by reference the general discussions and concentrating solely on the issues specific to the statement subsequently prepared." It also notes that tiering "is appropriate when it helps the lead agency to focus on the issues which are ripe for decision and exclude from consideration issues already decided or not yet ripe."

3.2.2 CEQ Guidance

The CEQ has addressed tiering in several guidance documents that were issued in the early 1980s. These guidance documents focused primarily on the use of tiering for programmatic analyses, not individual projects. They are summarized briefly below. For full text of the tiering sections of these documents, refer to Appendix B or the CEQ website at: http://ceq.hss.doe.gov/nepa/regs/guidance.html.

CEQ 40 Questions Guidance (1981). In this guidance, CEQ addressed tiering as it relates to NEPA studies for "plans, programs, or policies." The guidance distinguished between a Tier 1

---

[1] In a memorandum regarding the I-70 tiered project in Missouri, dated June 18, 2001, the FHWA stated that "…we could also foresee situations in which minor second tier actions qualified as categorical exclusions. (http://environment.transportation.org/pdf/programs/3-FHWA_Tiering_Memo_re_I-70_6-18-01.pdf). Additionally, in the Federal Register Notice of Intent for the Trans-Texas-Corridor 35 project, the FHWA stated that "Tier Two documents could be in the form of Environmental Assessments, Categorical Exclusions, or EISs depending upon the type, scope, and complexity of the proposed second tier projects." (Federal Register, Vol. 69, No. 24, Feb. 5, 2004). Environmental Assessments and Categorical Exclusions have been used as Tier 2 documentation for the Council Bluffs Interstate System Improvements and were also considered as part of the I-81 Corridor Improvement Study in Virginia.

study that encompasses a broad program and a series of Tier 2 "site specific or project-specific" studies. This guidance did not address the use of tiering for individual projects, such as highways.

CEQ Scoping Guidance (1981). This guidance emphasized that many stakeholders will be unfamiliar with tiering, so it is important for agencies to explain the tiered approach in the scoping process. The CEQ observed that "If tiering is being used, this concept must be made clear at the outset of any scoping meeting, so that participants do not concentrate on issues that are not going to be addressed at this time."

CEQ Memorandum to Federal Agencies (1983). This memorandum addressed issues associated with NEPA compliance and included a relatively lengthy discussion of tiering. Again, the CEQ focused primarily on the use of tiering for programmatic NEPA analyses. The guidance noted that the CEQ "regulations do not require tiering; rather, they authorize its use when an agency determines it is appropriate. It is an option for an agency to use when the nature of the proposal lends itself to tiered EIS(s)."

More recently, CEQ addressed the issue of tiering as part of its comprehensive NEPA Task Force report, "Modernizing NEPA Implementation," which was issued in September 2003. This report contained a chapter on "Programmatic Analysis and Tiering." However, this report focused mainly on tiering as a tool for NEPA compliance for agency programs. It did not address the use of tiering for individual projects.

3.2.3 FHWA and FTA Regulations

FHWA and FTA address the issue of tiering in their environmental review regulations (23 C.F.R. Part 771) and their regulations implementing Section 4(f) of the U.S. Department of Transportation Act (23 C.F.R. Part 774). These regulations provide more specific direction for applying a tiered approach to an individual highway or transit project. For the full text of these provisions, refer to Appendix C.

NEPA Regulations. In Section 771.111(g), FHWA and FTA note that tiering can be used for highway and transit projects and describe in general terms how a tiered environmental process would work:

> For major transportation actions, the tiering of EISs as discussed in the CEQ regulation (40 C.F.R. 1502.20) may be appropriate. The first tier EIS would focus on broad issues such as general location, mode choice, and areawide air quality and land use implications of the major alternatives. The second tier would address site-specific details on project impacts, costs, and mitigation measures.

Section 4(f) Regulations. In Section 774.7(e), FHWA and FTA explain how Section 4(f) requirements could be addressed in a tiered study. The regulations state that if detailed information needed to complete the Section 4(f) approval is not available during Tier 1, then the Tier 1 EIS should address "the potential impacts that a proposed action will have on Section 4(f) property and whether those impacts could have a bearing on the decision to be made." The Tier 1 EIS would then include a "preliminary Section 4(f) approval." In Tier 2, the Section 4(f) approval would be finalized. The regulations state that "Re-evaluation of the preliminary Section 4(f) approval is only needed to the extent that new or more detailed information available at the second-tier stage raises new Section 4(f) concerns not already considered."

3.2.4 FHWA Guidance

In 2001, FHWA provided recommendations for tiering in a memorandum directed to one specific study – the tiered EIS for improvements to I-70 in Missouri. This memorandum emphasizes that FHWA has "broad discretion" in deciding how to conduct a tiered study, and also notes that FHWA has "deliberately stayed away from prescriptive guidelines on how to apply tiering, so that each tiered process can be custom designed to the specific situation.... You therefore have considerable latitude in the specific tiering approach you utilize to implement the NEPA policy mandate of informed decision-making."

While emphasizing the broad flexibility that exists under the regulations, FHWA also provided several specific recommendations for the I-70 study. Many of these recommendations are applicable to tiered studies in general. Key recommendations include:

- FHWA should (1) explain the nature of the first and second tier decision-making so that affected parties are fully aware of their opportunities to influence outcomes at the various decision points and (2) structure the decisions to avoid, to the extent possible, a decision on one section forcing an undesirable outcome on another section.

- The Tier 2 studies can be Environmental Impact Statements, Environmental Assessments, or Categorical Exclusions, depending on the degree of impact.

- The Tier 1 Draft EIS should identify the proposed Tier 2 subsections (i.e., sections of independent utility) that will be the individual projects for which Tier 2 studies would be prepared if a Tier 1 ROD is issued. (Note: This recommendation was made in the context of a Tier 1 EIS for improvements to a 200-mile section of an existing Interstate. In other contexts, it may not be feasible to identify proposed Tier 2 projects in the Tier 1 Draft EIS.)

- The termini for the Tier 2 subsections should be defined by taking into account (1) the purpose and need for the subsection projects and (2) the need to avoid "pointing a loaded gun" at important resources beyond the terminus of that subsection.

- The Tier 2 analyses should "look beyond the subsection termini to adjacent subsections for which second tier analyses have not yet been undertaken" in order to ensure that one Tier 2 project does not point the "loaded gun" at resources associated with the adjacent Tier 2 project.

For the full text of the I-70 tiering memorandum, refer to Appendix D.

3.2.5 Other Statutes

While tiering is authorized under the NEPA and Section 4(f) regulations, it is not addressed in other statutes and regulations that play a key role in the environmental review process for transportation projects. As a result, there is no clear road-map for incorporating compliance with those other laws into a tiered NEPA process – and in some cases, agencies may have questions about whether they are authorized to carry out a tiered process. Key statutes to consider include the National Historic Preservation Act, Endangered Species Act, Clean Water Act, and Clean Air Act.

National Historic Preservation Act. Section 106 of the National Historic Preservation Act (NHPA) requires federal action agencies (e.g., FHWA, FTA, or FRA) to engage in consultation regarding the potential effects of a proposed action on historic resources listed in or eligible for the National Register of Historic Places. The Section 106 regulations (35 C.F.R. Part 800) do not specifically address the issue of how to conduct Section 106 compliance in a tiered NEPA process, nor has the Advisory Council on Historic Preservation (ACHP) issued guidance on this subject. The Section 106 regulations do authorize "phasing" of the identification of historic resources and the evaluation of effects (36 C.F.R. § 800.4(b)(2); § 800.5(a)(3)). The regulations state that phasing may be appropriate "where alternatives under consideration consist of corridors or large land areas" (36 C.F.R. § 800.4(b)(2)). When a phased approach is used, the initial phase focuses on determining the "likely presence" of historic properties and applying the adverse-effect criteria to the extent possible given those findings; the regulations note that documentation standards "should be applied flexibly" in these situations (36 C.F.R. § 800.4(b)(2); § 800.5(a)(3)). A phased approach provides a potential framework for initiating Section 106 consultation in Tier 1 and completing Section 106 consultation in Tier 2. It is important to note, however, that some tiered studies include Section 106 consultation only as part of the Tier 2 process.

Endangered Species Act. Section 7 of the Endangered Species Act (ESA) requires federal action agencies to engage in consultation regarding the potential effects of a proposed action on federally listed threatened and endangered species. The procedures for Section 7 consultation are defined in regulations issued by the U.S. Fish and Wildlife Service (USFWS). See 50 C.F.R. Part 402. These regulations do not specifically address the procedures for Section 7 consultation in a tiered NEPA study. The regulations do authorize an approach known as "incremental step" consultation, but that method has been largely limited to situations in which a federal action agency is required by statute to structure its decision in a series of incremental steps – which is rarely if ever the case with highways and other transportation projects. As a result, the USFWS's approach to tiering Section 7 consultation tends to be developed on a case-by-case basis. In some cases, USFWS will engage in full Section 7 consultation at Tier 1, resulting in a Tier 1 Biological Opinion, followed by more detailed project-specific consultation in Tier 2. In other cases, Section 7 consultation occurs only on a project-specific basis in Tier 2.

Clean Water Act. Section 404 of the Clean Water Act (CWA) prohibits any filling of wetlands or other discharges into waters of the United States without a permit. Section 404 permits are issued by the U.S. Army Corps of Engineers (ACOE), subject to a potential veto by the U.S. Environmental Protection Agency (EPA). The Corps has issued regulations (33 C.F.R. Part 325) that define the basic steps in the permitting process, while EPA has issued regulations – known as the Section 404(b)(1) Guidelines (40 C.F.R. Part 230) – that define the conditions under which a permit can be issued. Neither the Corps nor EPA has addressed the procedure for conducting Section 404 permitting in the context of a tiered NEPA study. One specific issue that often presents challenges in a tiered NEPA process is the timing of Section 404 permitting: Should a single Section 404 permit be issued for the entire project at the end of Tier 1? Or should Section 404 permitting be conducted for individual Tier 2 projects? If permitting is conducted solely at Tier 2, should Section 404 permitting requirements be considered at all in Tier 1? There is no guidance that directly addresses these issues, so they are resolved on a project-by-project basis.

Clean Air Act. Section 176(c) of the Clean Air Act (CAA) establishes air quality conformity requirements for transportation projects. Conformity requirements apply to projects in areas that have been designated as "nonattainment" or "maintenance" for specific air pollutants. FHWA and FTA can approve a project in a nonattainment or maintenance area only if the project "conforms to" the emissions budgets in the applicable State Implementation Plan. The EPA has issued regulations governing transportation conformity determinations (40 C.F.R. Part 93), but these regulations do not address conformity compliance in the context of tiered studies, nor have agencies issued guidance addressing these situations. In practice, FHWA has interpreted the conformity regulations to require a project-level conformity determination by the conclusion of Tier 2, not Tier 1 studies. (See Indiana I-69 case law discussion below.)

In addition to these statutes, there may be other federal, state, or local laws that must be considered as part of the environmental review process for a transportation project. In many cases, these other laws do not address tiering. Therefore, agencies involved in a tiered study must consider each of these other laws and make a project-specific decision about how the full range of non-NEPA requirements will be satisfied as part of a tiered NEPA process.

3.2.6 Case Law

The courts also have addressed tiering in several cases involving NEPA studies for highways and other linear projects. The case law recognizes that tiering is a valid approach for complying with NEPA, particularly for large-scale and complex plans, programs, and projects. The case law also recognizes that a Tier 1 EIS can be completed for a single large project, followed by a series of smaller-scale NEPA studies for individual sections or components of that project. The case law underscores the importance of considering NEPA and non-NEPA requirements when conducting a tiered study.

There is one recent case, *Hoosier Environmental Council v. USDOT,* in which a federal court addressed several challenges to a tiered NEPA study for a transportation project. This case involved the Tier 1 EIS and the Tier 1 Biological Opinion for the proposed I-69 project in Indiana. The U.S. District Court for the Southern District of Indiana issued a decision in December 2007, upholding the Tier 1 EIS and the Tier 1 Biological Opinion. The court considered the issue of tiering in detail and concluded that the level of detail in the Tier 1 EIS was appropriate:

> Tiering allows agencies contemplating projects of massive scope to sort through broad and far-reaching issues in an initial phase before expending the resources needed for more exacting determinations such as preparing engineering plans and acquiring rights-of-way in later phases....

> Here, INDOT and FHWA used tiering to gather information on twelve routes covering the southwestern quarter of Indiana before choosing one route to analyze at the level of detail necessary actually to build the road. The choice to analyze the impacts of such a large project in tiers was not arbitrary or capricious. If every major federal action required the level of analysis proposed for the second tier for every alternative considered, public works could too easily grind to a halt and become hopelessly mired in their own bureaucracy.... The art of effective tiering is to find the appropriate depth of detail at each level. Given the twenty-six county area studied for a highway ranging between 141 and 156 miles, the level of detail in the first tier selection of Alternative 3C was not arbitrary and capricious (*Hoosier Environmental Council v. USDOT,* 2007 U.S. Dist. LEXIS 90840 (Dec. 10, 2007), at *20-21).

The court in the I-69 case also noted tiering "does not come without significant risk." The court cited several potential risks in a tiered process:

- "Environmental impacts that appear to be tolerable and potentially manageable in the first tier may emerge as unacceptable threats to affected species and ecosystems during the more detailed scrutiny in the second tier."

- "[I]f tiering is not carefully coordinated and checked, it can enable agencies to abrogate or circumvent provisions of other environmental laws with substantive mandates and safeguards."

- "The agencies foresee those impacts as manageable and acceptable at this point. But after federal and state agencies conduct more detailed field studies along the Alternative 3C corridor and the agencies must face more detailed decisions about a more precise route, those impacts may or may not turn out to be acceptable. It is possible, although not probable given the information available, that INDOT and FHWA may have to return to the drawing board and reconsider previously rejected alternatives to achieve their goals. That possibility is, however, a risk inherent in, and not an abuse of, tiering."

- "Under the Clean Water Act, the Army Corps and EPA might end up agreeing with INDOT's and FHWA's determination that Alternative 3C is the most suitable route, but they also might not. The selection of preferred alternatives in the first tier provides no more than guidance on that issue and does not control the final determination under the Clean Water Act.... Acting agencies like FHWA and INDOT cannot lessen the obligations the Clean Water Act imposes on the Army Corps and the EPA by the use of tiering or through the selection of preferred alternatives. The Clean Water Act requires a rigorous level of environmental protection, though the use of tiering in this project means that the Clean Water Act protections will not be triggered until the agencies reach the second tier of analysis."

- "[T]he agencies have 'completed' formal [Section 7] consultation at the end of the first tier. No existing evidence indicates that the defendants will reinitiate formal consultation in the second tier. But it is possible that the Fish and Wildlife Service will re-initiate consultation based on information in the detailed surveys and field studies generated in the second tier. By that point, INDOT and FHWA may have irretrievably committed resources in some of the second tier segments.... [I]f the agencies re-initiate formal consultation that affects only a particular segment of I-69, the Endangered Species Act could require INDOT and FHWA to halt all irretrievable commitments of resources in any segment that would foreclose alternatives ensuring the continued existence of the Indiana bat and its habitat."

One other recent case, *Rivers Unlimited v. U.S. DOT*, also involved a challenge to a Tier 1 EIS (*Rivers Unlimited v. U.S. DOT*, 533 F.Supp.2d 1 (D.D.C. 2008)). That case involved the Eastern Corridor project, which included a proposed crossing of the Little Miami River on a highway connecting Cincinnati, Ohio, to its suburbs. While the case involved a tiered EIS, the court's decision did not address any tiering issues.

3.3 Related Legal Issues

Agencies considering tiering should also consider (1) the FHWA regulations and guidance on planning-NEPA linkage, which include a process that can be used instead of preparing a tiered EIS; and (2) the requirements of Section 6002 of SAFETEA-LU, which must be followed for all EISs initiated after the enactment of SAFETEA-LU (August 10, 2005).

3.3.1 FHWA/FTA Regulations and Guidance on Planning/NEPA Linkage

In February 2007, FHWA issued revised statewide and metropolitan planning regulations (23 C.F.R. Part 450) that provide a legal framework for using "corridor or subarea studies" in the planning process to resolve issues such as mode choice and corridor location. The regulations also include, in Appendix A, revised guidance on planning-NEPA linkage. The guidance explains in detail how the planning process can be used to resolve these issues.

The regulations allow corridor or subarea studies to be completed as part of the statewide planning process (23 C.F.R. § 450.212) or as part of the metropolitan planning process (23 C.F.R. § 450.318). The basic concept is the same in both processes: a study undertaken in the planning process can be used to produce any of the following for a transportation project:

(1) Purpose and need or goals and objective statement(s);

(2) General travel corridor and/or general mode(s) definition (e.g., highway, rail, transit) Preliminary screening of alternatives and elimination of unreasonable alternatives;

(3) Basic description of the environmental setting; and/or

(4) Preliminary identification of environmental impacts and environmental mitigation (23 C.F.R. § 450.212(a), § 450.318(a)).

The regulations allow FHWA or FTA to incorporate these products of the planning process in a subsequent NEPA document, if certain conditions are met. These conditions include:

(1) The NEPA lead agencies agree that such incorporation will aid in establishing or evaluating the purpose and need for the Federal action, reasonable alternatives, cumulative or other impacts on the human and natural environment, or mitigation of these impacts; and

(2) The systems-level, corridor, or subarea planning study is conducted with:

    (i)   Involvement of interested State, local, Tribal, and Federal agencies;

    (ii)   Public review;

    (iii)   Reasonable opportunity to comment during the metropolitan transportation planning process and development of the corridor or subarea planning study;

    (iv)   Documentation of relevant decisions in a form that is identifiable and available for review during the NEPA scoping process and can be appended to or referenced in the NEPA document; and

    (v)   The review of the FHWA and the FTA, as appropriate (23 C.F.R. § 450.212(b), § 450.318(b)).

The FHWA and FTA have discretion in the application of these criteria. As FHWA and FTA note in Appendix A to the planning regulations, "there are no guarantees" that the results of a planning study will be incorporated in a NEPA process. This uncertainty may lead some project sponsors to conclude that a Tier 1 EIS is preferable because it results in a federal decision (the Tier 1 Record of Decision), which provides greater finality than a planning study. Nonetheless, a planning study does provide one potential avenue for managing a large-scale project without preparing a tiered EIS.

3.3.2 Section 6002 Environmental Review Process

Section 6002 of SAFETEA-LU (23 U.S.C. § 139) established an "environmental review process" that is required to be followed for all environmental impact statements prepared for highway or transit projects that require approval of the U.S. Department of Transportation. FHWA has issued detailed guidance regarding implementation of Section 6002 (FHWA and FTA, "SAFETEA-LU Environmental Review Process Final Guidance" (Nov. 15, 2006), available at: http://www.fhwa.dot.gov/HEP/section6002/index.htm). The guidance clarifies that this process only applies to EISs initiated after the date of enactment of SAFETEA-LU, which was August 10, 2005.

Section 6002 establishes an overall framework for complying with NEPA as well as environmental review and permitting requirements under other laws. The U.S. DOT is defined as the lead agency in this process; the project sponsor also serves as a lead agency. Key steps in the Section 6002 process include: (1) inviting "participating agencies," (2) developing a "coordination plan" that defines procedures for working with those agencies, (3) providing an opportunity for agency and public involvement in defining the purpose and need and the range of alternatives, and (4) collaborating with participating agencies in determining the level of detail and methodologies used for studying alternatives. The Section 6002 process also includes other requirements, including comment deadlines and procedures for resolving issues that could delay needed approvals.

In the Section 6002 guidance, FHWA and FTA have specifically addressed the application of Section 6002 to tiered studies:

> The SAFETEA-LU requirements do apply to Tier 1 EISs. The NEPA regulations of USDOT and CEQ permit the tiering of EISs (23 C.F.R. 771.111(g) and 40 C.F.R. 1502.02). The first tier EIS would address broad issues in the study area, such as the effectiveness of complementary transportation actions of various modes and general locations in alleviating the transportation problems in the study area. The initiation of a first tier EIS does trigger the SAFETEA-LU requirements. However, the description of the "type of work" and other information for project initiation (see Question 11), the impact assessment methodologies, the corresponding coordination plan with participating agencies, and other features of the review process will reflect the broader level of decisionmaking at the Tier 1 planning phase. When the lead agencies initiate Tier 2 proceedings, the SAFETEA-LU requirements will apply, but procedures and documentation should be adapted as appropriate to reflect the results of the Tier 1 proceedings.

While this guidance is not prescriptive, it does confirm that Section 6002 requirements must be followed in tiered studies for highway and transit projects. The Section 6002 guidance also confirms that a 180-day statute of limitations can be issued for a Tier 1 ROD (FHWA and FTA,

"SAFETEA-LU Environmental Review Process Final Guidance" (Nov. 15, 2006), Appendix E, Question E-14).

3.4 Pros and Cons of Tiering

As the court recognized in the I-69 case, tiering can provide additional flexibility and efficiency in the NEPA process for a large-scale project, but it also carries potentially significant risks. The basic pros and cons of tiering include:

3.4.1 Pros

- May be the only feasible way to manage the NEPA process for extremely large-scale projects.

- Allows for a wide range of alternatives to be considered in the NEPA process (in Tier 1), while also allowing for in-depth consideration of local issues (in Tier 2).

- Facilitates consideration of indirect and cumulative impacts on a broad scale – for example, an indirect and cumulative impacts analysis could be included in a Tier 1 study and then incorporated by reference in individual Tier 2 studies.

- Increases opportunities for agency and public involvement, because they are engaged in broad decisions about the basic project concept and location (Tier 1) and are engaged again about detailed siting and mitigation issues (Tier 2).

- Allows timing of final NEPA approval (Tier 2) to be more closely correlated with actual timing of project construction, because Tier 2 studies can be completed over time as construction funding becomes available.

- Provides a framework for integrating transportation planning with comprehensive land use or natural resource planning efforts, because a Tier 1 EIS may be more compatible than following a traditional EIS process with the timing and level of detail of land use and resource planning studies.

- Can support corridor preservation, except where prohibited by state law, because the Tier 1 ROD may allow for the use of Federal funding to purchase ROW.

- In Tier 2, issues which may delay the progress of one Tier 2 section will not delay the entire project as progress can still be made on the other Tier 2 sections.

3.4.2 Cons

- Requires customization, because there is no standard "off the shelf" process for tiering. Customization takes time and requires attention of agency leadership.

- Requires extensive efforts to educate and explain the tiered process to agencies and the public. Even with those efforts, tiering could become a focal point for agency and public concerns.

- May need to conduct more detailed work in Tier 1 than initially planned. Increasing the level of detail in Tier 1 can undermine one of the key benefits of the tiered process: considering indirect and cumulative impacts on a broad scale.

- May have difficulty reaching agreement among agencies with jurisdiction on how to handle non-NEPA requirements in a tiered NEPA process. For example, there could be disagreements among agencies on how to incorporate Section 404 permitting, ESA consultation, or Section 106 consultation into a tiered NEPA process.

- Difficult to achieve complete finality, even after a Tier 1 ROD is issued. Preparing a Tier 1 Reevaluation or Supplemental EIS has the potential to delay or otherwise complicate ongoing Tier 2 studies for individual project sections.

- Once a tiered study has been successfully completed, it may create the expectation, with resource agencies and the public, that all future transportation projects should use the tiered environmental process.

4 State of the Practice and Managing Risk

In recent years, FHWA, FTA, and FRA have initiated tiered environmental impact statements for a wide range of projects. Some of those tiered studies have been completed successfully, others are still under way, and a few have been placed on hold, terminated, or converted to traditional non-tiered studies. In addition, tiered NEPA studies were initiated during this period by the Federal Aviation Administration, Federal Motor Carrier Safety Administration, and the Surface Transportation Board. This study focused on roadway and passenger rail transportation. Therefore, while other transportation agency (FAA, FMCSA, and STB) studies were identified, they were not investigated further as part of this report.

4.1 Research for this Guide

To gain insight into the practice and strategies for managing risk, the study team gathered information from 25 tiered NEPA studies that were initiated since 1999. The 25 studies investigated were selected to represent a cross-section of those projects, taking into account geographic location, mode, lead agency, project scale, and environmental and regulatory issues. The study methodology and results are documented in a technical report that is included as part of this guidance (Appendix F).

4.2 How Tiering Has Been Used

Tiering has been used for a wide range of highway, transit, and rail projects in the past nine years. Table 4-1 summarizes the Tier 1 and Tier 2 EISs the FHWA, FTA, and FRA have undertaken and Appendix E provides more detail. This information demonstrates the volume and diversity of tiered studies initiated. Please note that Table 4-1 includes Tier 1 and Tier 2 EISs. In addition to the studies presented in Table 4-1, several Tier 2 studies were completed as Categorical Exclusions or Environmental Assessments. There is no single repository for locating information on Categorical Exclusions or Environmental Assessments because they do not require publishing an NOI in the Federal Register. As a result, they were not included in this report.

Reasons for Tiering. Tiering was adopted for three main reasons: (1) complexity of managing the NEPA process for lengthy corridors; (2) desire to authorize corridor preservation, where construction is not anticipated for many years; and (3) lack of funding to complete a traditional EIS which would require studies that are more detailed than is typically required for a Tier 1 EIS. Another reason for tiering (that usually coincides with a lack of funding) is to prevent the numerous studies associated with a traditional EIS from becoming outdated because the funding shortage prevents the project from moving forward.

Geographic Region. Tiered EISs have been undertaken for surface transportation projects in every geographic region and for projects in both rural and metropolitan areas. The tiered process was initiated for 60 projects between 1999 and September 2008. California has initiated the most tiered studies (11). Other States that have used tiering (for highway, transit, and/or rail modes) include Colorado, Georgia (including one multi-state between Georgia and Tennessee), Florida, Indiana, Louisiana, Missouri, Maryland (including one multi-state with the District of Columbia), Minnesota, New York, South Carolina, Texas, Virginia, and Washington.

Mode and Lead Agency. The FHWA, FTA, and FRA all initiated tiered studies. The FHWA has initiated 40 tiered studies, the FRA has initiated 11 and the FTA has initiated four. In

Table 4-1: Tier1 and Tier 2 EISs Initiated Since 1999 by FHWA, FTA, FRA or Jointly[23]

FHWA	FTA	FRA	Co-Lead Tiered EIS Projects
• I-70 – Jackson County – MO/KS State Line to I-470 Interchange (incl. Kansas City Downtown) (MO) – Tier 1	• Transit Improvements in Beltline Corridor, Atlanta (GA) – Tier 1	• Southeast High Speed Rail Corridor – Petersburg, VA to Raleigh, NC (VA, NC) – Tier 1	• Atlanta to Chattanooga High Speed Ground Transportation (GA, TN) – Tier 1; FHWA and FRA
• SR 180 Westside Expressway – Fresno County (CA) – Tier 1; FHWA assigned Caltrans NEPA lead.	• Jacksonville Rapid Transit System (FL) – Tier 1	• Southeast High Speed Rail Corridor – Washington, DC to Raleigh, NC (DC, NC)– Tier 1	• Tappan Zee Bridge/I-287(NY) – Tier 1; FHWA and FTA
• I-70 Improvements (MO) – Supplement to Tier 1 and Tier 2	• South Florida East Coast Corridor Transit Analysis (FL) – Tier 1	• Southeast High Speed Rail – Richmond to Raleigh – (VA, NC) – Tier 2	• I-405 Improvements (WA) – Tier 1; FHWA and FTA
• SR 25 San Benito and Santa Clara Counties (CA) – Tier 1; FHWA assigned Caltrans NEPA lead.	• Long Island Railroad – Huntington/Port Jefferson Branch Yard (NY) – Tier 2	• High Speed Rail Corridor –Las Vegas to Anaheim (CA, NV) – Tier 1 and Tier 2	
• Baton Rouge Loop (LA) – Tier 1		• High Speed Rail Corridor – Richmond to Hampton Roads (VA) – Tier 1	
• Elgin O'Hare-West Bypass (IL) – Tier 1		• Passenger Rail Improvements – Los Angeles to San Diego (CA) – Tier 1	
• US 220 from I-68 in MD to Corridor H in WV (MD, WV) – Tier 1		• California High Speed Train System (CA) – Tier 1	
• US 50 Corridor – Pueblo to Kansas State Line (CO)– Tier 1		• Bay Area to Central Valley High Speed Trail (CA) – Tier 1 (tiered under first Tier 1 above)	
• Lafayette Metropolitan Expressway (LA) – Tier 1		• California High Speed Rail System (CA) – Los Angeles to Orange County – Tier 2	
• Newberg Dundee Bypass (OR) – Tier 2		• California High Speed Train System (CA) – Palmdale to	
• I-73 Hamlet NC to I-95 in SC - (SC) – Tier 1; converted to non-tiered EIS.			
• I-73 State line to I-95 in SC – (NC, SC) – Tier 1			
• I-69 Evansville to Indianapolis (IN) – Tier 1			
• I-69 Section 1 (Evansville			

[2] Please note that this table includes environmental Tier 1 and Tier 2 EISs. In addition to these studies, a number of Tier 1 CEs and EAs have been prepared, but were not studied as part of this report.

[3] The California High Speed Rail System (CA) – San Francisco to San Jose – Tier 2, was initiated after our research was completed. The NOI was published on Dec. 29th, 2008. (http://www.cahighspeedrail.ca.gov/images/chsr/20090113113851_Federal%20NOI.pdf)

FHWA	FTA	FRA	Co-Lead Tiered EIS Projects
to Oakland City) (IN) – Tier 2 • I-69 Section 2 (Oakland City to Washington) (IN) – Tier 2 • I-69 Section 3 (Washington to US 231) (IN) – Tier 2 • I-69 Section 4 (US 231 to Bloomington) (IN) – Tier 2 • I-69 Section 5 (Bloomington to Martinsville) (IN) – Tier 2 • I-69 Section 6 (Martinsville to Indianapolis) (IN) – Tier 2 • TTC-35 (TX) – Tier 1 • I-69 Trans Texas Corridor (TX) – Tier 1 • I-81 (VA)– Tier 1 • Placer Parkway Corridor Preservation (CA) – Tier 1 • TH-10 (MN) – Tier 1; terminated. • TH-41 (MN) – Tier 1 • Arterial Connecting TH-15 to TH10 including River Crossing, St. Cloud (MN) – Tier 1 • I-80, I-29, and I-490 Council Bluffs (NE, IA) – Tier 1 • M-59 Widening from I-96 to U.S. 23 (MI)– Tier 1 • Eastern Corridor (OH, KY) – Tier 1 • US 10 (WI) – Tier 1 • Hemet to Corona East-West Transportation Corridor Riverside County (CA) – Tier 1 • SR 520 Corridor Seattle to Redmond (WA) – Tier 1 • US 301 Southern Corridor – Prince Georges County (MD) – Tier 1 and 2		Los Angeles – Tier 2 • Maglev Deployment Program – Tier 1 • Baltimore to Washington DC Maglev (DC, MD) – Tier 2 • Pennsylvania Maglev (PA) – Tier 2	

FHWA	FTA	FRA	Co-Lead Tiered EIS Projects
• I-70 Mountain Corridor (CO) – Tier 1 • I-70 Improvements (MO) – Tier 1 • I-70 Montgomery City to Lake St. Louis (MO) – Tier 2 • I-70 Boone County (MO) – Tier 2 • I-90 Snoqualmie Pass (WA) – Tier 1 • Winchester to Temecula North-South Transportation Corridor (CA) – Tier 1 • State Route 11 and the Otay Mesa East Port of Entry (CA) – Tier 1			

Sources: Federal Registers, Parsons Brinckerhoff, and Perkins Coi, 2008.

addition, two tiered studies were co-lead by the FHWA and FTA and one was co-lead by the FHWA and FRA.

Scale of Project/Study Area. Tiering was used for projects of widely varying lengths. Several of the Tier 1 EISs included corridors of 200 miles or longer. The longest corridor considered in a Tier 1 study was the I-69 project in Texas (approximately 1,000 miles). Other lengthy corridors considered in Tier 1 studies included TTC-35 in Texas (800 miles); California High Speed Train System (700 miles); Southeast High Speed Rail System in Virginia and North Carolina (477 miles); I-81 in Virginia (325 miles); and I-70 in Missouri (200 miles). Tiering also was used for several much shorter projects. For example, Tier 1 EISs were initiated for State Route 25 in California (11 miles), Placer Parkway in California (15 miles); M-59 Widening in Michigan (13 miles); and I-90 Snoqualmie Pass in Washington State (13 miles). Scale can also be defined by the geographic size of the study area.

Range of Alternatives. For projects where the mode had been determined, the Tier 1 EIS typically focused on determining a general location – often called a corridor – for the entire project, as well as resolving certain basic features of the transportation facility, such as interchange locations and a standard cross-section. The "corridor" for some alternatives may also be a network of corridors (i.e., E-W and N-S components). For projects where the mode had not been determined, the Tier 1 EIS typically included consideration of modal alternatives as well as location alternatives. The need to consider multiple modes added to the complexity (and often the time) needed to complete the Tier 1 study.

Level of Detail. Tiered studies varied greatly in the level of detail conducted at Tier 1 and Tier 2. Some Tier 1 studies rely primarily on existing information and are similar to pre-NEPA planning studies in their level of detail. Others involve extensive field work and approach the level of detail included in some non-tiered EISs. Factors affecting the level of detail in Tier 1 include: (1) overall size of the study area and length of the alternatives; (2) the complexity of the environmental issues present in the study area; (3) the information required to satisfy non-NEPA requirements, including requirements involving other agencies, such as Section 404 permitting; and (4) the amount of funding available for the Tier 1 study. The Tier 2 studies generally involve the level of detail for any non-tiered EIS, but tend to be more streamlined because they consider a relatively narrow range of alternatives and often focus on a smaller geographic area – e.g., a specific section of the corridor approved in the Tier 1 study.

Regulatory Compliance. Some tiered studies included steps to comply with regulatory requirements – Section 106, Section 7, etc. – as part of the Tier 1 study, while others complied with these requirements as part of the Tier 2 studies. For example, the Tier 1 EIS for I-69 study in Indiana included Section 7 consultation with the USFWS, resulting in a Tier 1 Biological Opinion that was included in the Tier 1 Final EIS. Other Tier 1 studies specifically stated that Section 7 consultation would be addressed as part of Tier 2.

Schedule. It is difficult to draw firm conclusions from this study about the length of time needed to complete a tiered process, because many of the studies are still under way. In addition, because tiering is sometimes adopted because a lead agency lacks funding to complete a traditional EIS, the limited funding can result in delays in completing the NEPA process, so delays are not necessarily attributable to tiering itself. Nonetheless, anecdotal evidence suggests that Tier 1 studies often take longer than initially anticipated. See Table 4-1. In addition, after the Tier 1 process is completed, the agencies must still complete one or more Tier 2 studies. Therefore, while tiering may expedite the resolution of broad issues such as mode and corridor, the total time needed to complete all NEPA studies for a project is likely to be longer with tiering than with a single non-tiered NEPA study.

4.3 Common Risks in Tiered Studies

Tiering can be the best tool for managing the NEPA process for unusually lengthy or complex transportation projects. The principal advantage of tiering – when it works well – is that tiering makes it possible to address a broad range of alternatives across a large geographic area, and then lock in a decision about a specific corridor and route for the entire project, while deferring some time-intensive tasks until a later time when individual sections of the project are built. This approach strikes a balance between two important goals in the NEPA process: considering environmental issues on a broad scope, while also ensuring that sufficient attention is given to site-specific details and mitigation measures in each affected community.

Despite these benefits, tiering also presents some risks that are not present (or present to a lesser degree) in a traditional non-tiered NEPA process. These include:

"Scope Creep." The initial plans for a Tier 1 scope can expand over time, resulting in "scope creep" – a gradual increase in the level of detail developed as part of the Tier 1 EIS. Scope creep can occur for many reasons. In some cases, the initial scope was not well-defined or did not include specific tasks that were needed to allow for informed decision-making in the Tier 1 process. In other cases, the gradual increase in the level of detail may occur as a way of resolving disagreements with resource agencies and allowing the process to keep moving. As the level of detail increases, the Tier 1 EIS may begin to approximate a non-tiered EIS in level of detail. When this occurs, the benefits of tiering are reduced. Tiering could end up being more time-consuming than a non-tiered NEPA study.

Distrust of Tiered Process. The tiered process can be viewed by agencies and stakeholders as a means of deferring consideration of sensitive issues until it is too late for meaningful involvement. In those cases, the tiered approach can become controversial and can even become the subject of litigation.

Difficulty Resolving Section 4(f) Issues. The Section 4(f) regulations outline the basic approach to Section 4(f) compliance in a tiered study: a preliminary Section 4(f) approval is granted at Tier 1, and that approval is finalized as part of Tier 2 studies. But in practice, Section 4(f) issues can be challenging to address in a tiered study. Potentially difficult issues include: determining how much effort is needed in Tier 1 to identify and evaluate historic resources, whose eligibility status and boundaries may be difficult to estimate without detailed investigations; determining the prudence and feasibility of avoidance alternatives, which may be difficult to assess without detailed engineering and environmental information; and determining whether de minimis findings are appropriate, which also can be difficult to assess without detailed engineering and environmental information. These risks can be managed by increasing the level of effort in Tier 1, but that approach can lead to the "scope creep" noted above.

Uncertainty about Process/Timing for Section 404 Permitting. Most large transportation projects involve some impacts on waters of the U.S. and therefore require permitting under Section 404 of the Clean Water Act. A critical issue in the Section 404 permitting process is the determination of the least environmentally damaging practicable alternative (LEDPA). Interpretations differ about whether a LEDPA determination should be made at Tier 1 (for the project as a whole) or for individual Tier 2 projects. There is no well-established approach to handling LEDPA issues in tiered studies. If agencies cannot agree on how to handle LEDPA issues, those disagreements can become a significant source of delay.

Uncertainty about Process/Timing for Section 7 Consultation. If a project has potential impacts on threatened or endangered species, Section 7 consultation under the Endangered Species Act (ESA) will be required. The potential for ESA consultation presents several risks. First, there is the potential for disagreement about when consultation should be initiated and, more generally, how ESA consultation should be melded with the tiered NEPA process. Disagreements on these procedural issues can lead to delays. Second, there is potential disagreement about the appropriate level of effort *under the ESA* at Tier 1. Third, even if the Tier 1 investigations are thorough, there is the potential that Tier 2 studies will identify new issues that require reevaluation of Tier 1 studies and/or Tier 1 decisions.

Potential to "Re-Open" Tier 1 After Tier 2 is Under Way. The basic goal of any Tier 1 study is to resolve certain fundamental issues – typically including the mode and corridor for a transportation project. In general, Tier 1 decisions are treated as a "given" in Tier 2, and the Tier 2 studies focus on how to implement those decisions. But if new issues arise after the completion of the Tier 1 study, it may be necessary to consider preparing a Supplemental Tier 1 EIS (SEIS). The preparation of a Tier 1 SEIS could delay initiation of the Tier 2 studies. If the Tier 2 studies are already under way, the lead agencies would have to decide whether to place those studies on hold pending completion of the Tier 1 SEIS, or move forward with the Tier 1 SEIS and Tier 2 studies in parallel with one another. With any of these approaches, the preparation a Tier 1 SEIS is likely to delay completion of the tiered NEPA process.

4.4 Factors Associated with Success in Tiered Studies

In many respects, the factors associated with the success of a tiered NEPA study are similar to those associated with the success of any NEPA study – regardless of whether tiering is used. These factors include: strong support from elected officials and the public; sufficient funding for the study and the project; a cohesive and well-managed project team; early coordination with resource and regulatory agencies; effective stakeholder involvement; effective integration of the NEPA process with review and permitting requirements under other laws; and an ability to adapt to changing circumstances. When these factors are present, there is a strong chance that any NEPA study will be successful.

While these common factors exist, several specific factors are especially important in the context of a tiered NEPA process. These include:

Good "Fit" Between Project and Tiered Process. Tiering is not the appropriate tool for every project. Tiering generally works best for projects where (1) the basic project definition is clear, and (2) the scale of the project is so large that it would be difficult to complete the entire NEPA process and related environmental reviews in a single study. Tiering is less well-suited for:

- *Projects that are capable of being handled efficiently in a single non-tiered NEPA document.* Tiering is sometimes used for relatively small-scale (10 to 20 mile) projects, which fall well within the range of projects that are typically studied in a non-tiered NEPA process. Often, tiering is adopted for these projects for corridor preservation because construction funding is not yet available and there is a desire to undertake a lower-cost EIS as a basis for preserving right-of-way. While this approach can work, the complexity of developing a tiered approach often offsets any anticipated cost or time savings in those cases.

- *Situations in which the transportation planning process has not yet resolved fundamental modal choice issues.* Tiering is sometimes used as a method for comparing alternative modes to one another (e.g., highway vs. rail or highway vs. transit) in a corridor. When mode choice is a main focus of the study (not just a screening issue), the tiered study becomes significantly more complex. The study team would likely include multiple lead agencies, such as FHWA and FTA. The alternatives analysis would need to compare modes to one another, as well as comparing alternatives within each mode. This added complexity greatly increases the difficulty of managing the NEPA process. The statewide and metropolitan planning process includes tools (e.g., corridor and subarea studies) that may be more appropriate for resolving modal choice issues.

Well-Defined Decision-Making Process. The essence of tiering is that *decision-making* occurs in two (or more) stages. As the CEQ regulations state, a tiered process is appropriate when it "helps the lead agency to focus on the issues which are ripe for decision and exclude from consideration issues already decided or not yet ripe." The foundation of a successful tiered study is a clear distinction between Tier 1 and Tier 2 decisions. If the lead agencies do not clearly identify the decisions to be made at Tier 1, there is no basis for determining the appropriate level of detail for the Tier 1 studies. Conversely, if the decisions to be made in Tier 1 are clearly defined, those decisions become the "driver" for deciding what information needs to be developed as part of the Tier 2 study.

High-Level Involvement and Support. A tiered study is not a routine study. Rather than following standard operating procedures, it requires those procedures to be customized. Customization requires decision-making by agency leadership. Therefore, even more than most EISs, a tiered EIS requires a commitment by agency leadership to provide consistent attention and support for the study team. This is especially important for the lead agency and the project sponsor, but high-level involvement also will be needed from other federal or state agencies that have a significant permitting or consultation role – e.g., the Corps of Engineers when a Section 404 permit will be needed for the project.

Well-Defined Tiering Work Plans. A tiered process requires many judgments to be made about what analysis should be done in Tier 1 and what should be done in Tier 2. In many cases, there can be significant differences of opinion about "how much is enough" in Tier 1. In successful tiered studies, the project sponsors address this issue up-front by developing detailed outlines of Tier 1 and Tier 2 tasks. One option is to develop a "Work Plan" that summarizes the Tier 1 and Tier 2 tasks for each major topic in the NEPA process – air quality, wetlands, noise, etc. This work plan would address not only the technical activities to be completed at each tier, but also the agency consultation and permitting-related activities. The basis for determining the level of detail in Tier 1 is the nature of the *decision* to be made at that stage.

Early Agency Involvement. Early resource agency involvement is a key factor in the success of a tiered study. Rather than developing a tiered approach and then presenting it as a done deal, it is helpful for project sponsors and lead agencies to involve the resource agencies in making several fundamental decisions: Is tiering a good fit for this project? How would a tiered approach work? In particular, what would tiering mean for each individual resource agency's responsibilities under its own laws and regulations? Addressing these issues through a collaborative approach can help build resource agency support for tiering, as well as building their understanding of the specifics of the tiered approach.

Effective Public Outreach and Education. Even with a non-tiered study, the NEPA process can be difficult for the general public to understand. A tiered study introduces a new layer of complexity and increases the potential for misunderstanding and mistrust. If the project is already controversial, tiering can become a target for public concerns. Therefore, a critical factor in the success of any tiered study is early, effective communication with the public. This often requires a sustained outreach effort – not just a one-time event – to communicate the essential elements of the tiered approach. Simplicity is key: the public involvement materials should clearly and succinctly describe the steps in the tiered process, highlighting key decision points and opportunities for public involvement.

Funding Availability. Tiered EISs are inherently challenging, but the challenges can grow exponentially if funding for the study is provided intermittently, or insufficient for necessary study tasks to be completed. Where funding is intermittent, the process tends to follow a "start/stop/re-start" cycle, with periods of intense activity interspersed by periods when the project is on hold. This pattern can be challenging for any EIS, but is especially challenging for a tiered EIS because the periods of inactivity compound the difficulty of communicating the tiered approach to agencies and the public. Therefore, one key to a successful tiered study is ensuring that sufficient funding for the EIS is available when the EIS is initiated.

5   Checklist of Issues to Consider

5.1   Whether to Tier

There are many situations in which a lead agency considers the possibility of tiering, and then decides to proceed with a different approach – sometimes a non-tiered NEPA process, sometimes a pre-NEPA planning study, and sometimes no study at all. The decision about whether to tier is a crucial decision and deserves careful consideration. The following questions identify some key factors to consider in deciding whether tiering is a good decision for your project.

- *Is the project ready for NEPA review? Or could additional study in the transportation planning process help to further refine issues of location and mode choice?*

  The statewide and metropolitan transportation planning process provides a framework for resolving issues of general location and mode choice. In many cases, these issues can be resolved by preparing a "corridor or subarea study," which would include many of the same elements as a Tier 1 EIS, but would be less time-consuming to complete. See 23 C.F.R. § 450.212 and 450.318, and Part 450 Appendix A. A corridor or sub-area study could help to reduce the range of geographic and/or modal alternatives under consideration. Even if a tiered EIS is still needed, the pre-NEPA planning process can help to produce a more focused and efficient NEPA study.

- *What decisions are ripe to be made?*

  If there is no consensus regarding the "big picture" among stakeholders at the planning process outset, tiering may be an appropriate choice. The corridor location and basic transportation concept may be an important first step in building consensus, and resolving the "big picture." A tiered process can serve to focus stakeholders on defining transportation needs and a thorough review of project alternatives, rather than getting bogged down in detailed engineering considerations that are not ripe for a decision. Tiering can also provide finality to that "big picture" consensus with a FEIS and ROD.

- *What are the trade-offs with pursuing a Tiered versus a traditional non-tiered NEPA process?*

  If a project can be completed efficiently with a non-tiered NEPA process, that is usually the best approach. By its nature, a tiered process involves a higher degree of customization; additional lead agency (FHWA, FRA, FTA) resources are needed to define the tiered process, educate resources agencies (USACE, USEPA, USFWS, etc…) and the public, and resolve tiering-related issues that arise during the study. This investment of resources is only warranted if there are substantial off-setting benefits. The most compelling reason to initiate a tiered study is that a non-tiered NEPA process simply is not workable given the scale of the proposed action.

- *Is there strong support for tiering among the lead agency and project sponsor?*

  Tiering will require high-level attention from the lead agency and the project sponsor. Lead agency leadership must understand the tiered process and be willing to "champion" the process in communications with other agencies and stakeholder. If there is not strong support for tiering at the leadership level of the project sponsor and lead agency, it is far less likely that the tiered approach will be successful.

- *Is a well-defined tiering work plan in place?*

  The best time to prepare a detailed work plan is before issuing a Notice of Intent to prepare a tiered EIS. The work plan will define the basic elements of the tiered process – the decisions to be made, the analysis and data gathering activities, and the agencies involved. Lead agency leadership should have at least a basic work plan in hand before making a decision to proceed with a tiered EIS.

- *Do the agencies involved have prior experience with tiering for transportation projects?*

  Tiered studies have been prepared for a wide range of transportation projects since 1999. This increasing body of experience means that many transportation and environmental agencies have now had some recent experience with tiering. If it was positive, it could help build support for undertaking another tiered study. If it was not positive, that experience could create a strong resistance to tiering. It is essential to understand this context before making a commitment to prepare a tiered EIS.

- *Is sufficient funding available to carry out the Tier 1 study, including an appropriate allowance for unanticipated tasks that could extend the duration of the Tier 1 EIS?*

  Overall, tiering may be a cost-effective approach for a complex project, but the cost of preparing a Tier 1 EIS can be significant. If funding is provided only in small increments, there is a much greater risk that the tiered process will be unsuccessful or at least fall short of the project sponsor's desired timeline. For tiering to be successful, it is preferable to begin with a realistic budget and sufficient funding in place to complete the Tier 1 study.

5.2 How to Tier

The decision about *whether to tier* is inextricably linked to the decision about *how to tier*, because a lead agency will want to define the tiering work plan in some detail before making a commitment to proceed with tiering. Therefore, the questions below should be considered by an agency contemplating the possibility of tiering. They also should be considered once a decision has been made to tier, because they will help to refine the work plan for the tiered study.

5.2.1 Decisions to Be Made in Tier 1

As a starting point for developing a tiered approach, it is useful to ask: *What decisions do we hope to make at the end of the Tier 1 study?* For transportation projects, the Tier 1 study is most often used to resolve the basic project concept (mode or combination of modes) and general location (corridors). In a Tier 1 study, locations for proposed alternatives are often defined as "corridors." In most cases, the corridors considered in a Tier 1 study are substantially wider than the right-of-way that is expected to be needed for the project. Selecting a corridor in Tier 1 leaves flexibility for specific alignments to be determined in Tier 2, when a higher degree of engineering detail is available. Consistent with this practice, the term "corridor" is used below in describing potential Tier 1 alternatives.

It is helpful to be as specific as possible about these goals. The following questions may help to fine-tune the decisions to be made in Tier 1.

- *Is this study intended to resolve a choice among modes?*

  Many tiered EISs focus primarily on a specific mode. For example, the FTA has prepared Tier 1 EISs on transit projects, and the FRA has prepared them for high-speed rail projects. In a few cases, Tier 1 EISs have been used to resolve fundamental modal-choice issues that were not resolved in the statewide or metropolitan planning process. If the Tier 1 EIS is being used to resolve mode choice, it is important to structure the study accordingly. For example, the lead agencies should (in most cases) include the modal agencies with responsibility for each mode that is being considered. The project schedule, the scoping process, and the corridor alternatives analysis should all be structured to allow for resolution of modal choice and project corridor location decisions.

- *What is the width of the "corridor" that will be studied in Tier 1?*

  There is no standard corridor width for Tier 1 studies, as NEPA only provides a framework for the planning process. For the I-69 project in Indiana, the Tier 1 corridor was approximately 2,000 feet wide. For the TH 41 project in Minnesota, the Tier 1 corridor was approximately 300 feet wide. For the I-69/Trans-Texas Corridor project, the Tier 1 corridor was 4 miles wide. Also, while there may be a standard width for the Tier 1 corridor, it is possible to vary the width depending on project features, topography, environmental resources, or other factors.

- *Will there be flexibility to shift outside the selected corridor in Tier 2?*

  In general, the goal of Tier 1 is to resolve the corridor location. However, agencies and the public may be concerned about unidentified resources within the selected corridor. Some projects, such as I-69 in Indiana, allow some flexibility to shift outside the corridor in Tier 2 if unanticipated issues arise.

- *Will right-of-way acquisition be authorized in Tier 1? If so, to what extent?*

  One possible objective of a tiered study is to begin acquiring right-of-way for a project. The Tier 1 EIS could be used as the basis for FHWA (or other agencies) to approve full acquisition of right-of-way for the entire project. This would depend upon both the width of the corridor, as well as whether state law would prohibit this type of property acquisition. Alternatively, the Tier 1 EIS could be used for the more limited purpose of authorizing hardship and protective acquisitions (which also could be authorized with individual categorical exclusions). The level of authorization desired may influence the corridor width used in the Tier 1 study.

- *Will mitigation be authorized in Tier 1?*

  Agencies increasingly consider early implementation of mitigation commitments as a way to demonstrate environmental stewardship and build support for a project. A Tier 1 ROD could include specific authorization to use federal funds for mitigation measures that will apply to the overall project, including sections that will not immediately move forward into Tier 2 studies. Similarly, Section 6001 of SAFETEA-LU (23 U.S.C. § 134, 135) requires that a discussion of potential environmental mitigation activities occur as part of the metropolitan and statewide long-range plans between the Federal, State, and regulatory agencies.

- *Will the Tier 1 ROD define the termini/scope of Tier 2 projects?*

  Most tiered studies for lengthy corridor projects involve a single Tier 1 EIS followed by a series of Tier 2 studies for sub-sections of the corridor covered in Tier 1. In its guidance for the I-70 project, FHWA recommended that the Tier 1 Draft EIS identify the proposed termini for the Tier 2 sub-sections. For this project, the Missouri DOT and FHWA identified in the Tier 1 ROD the termini of seven Tier 2 sections of independent utility. These seven sub-sections were each successfully studied in Tier 2. This guidance seems to assume that the Tier 1 ROD will identify and approve the termini for the Tier 2 subsections. In practice, the termini for Tier 2 subsections are sometimes identified in other documents. For example, the Tier 2 termini for the Southeast High Speed Rail Project were identified in a "Draft Implementation Plan" issued the same month as the Tier 1 ROD.

5.2.2 Level of Detail in Tier 1

The information in the Tier 1 EIS must be sufficient to allow for an informed decision on the issues that will be resolved in the Tier 1 ROD. For example, if the project sponsor hopes to resolve the location of a bridge through a wetland in Tier 1, the Tier 1 EIS would need to include sufficient detail to allow for an accurate assessment of Section 404 permitting requirements. If it is not feasible or desirable to develop that information, the tiered process could be structured so that avoidance alternatives for that wetland are preserved until Tier 2. Thus, the decisions being made in Tier 1 are the fundamental "driver" of the level of detail that needs to be included in a Tier 1 EIS. The following specific issues should be considered in determining the appropriate level of detail for the Tier 1 study:

- *How will the alternatives be defined in Tier 1? What level of engineering will be performed?*

  An "alternative" in a Tier 1 EIS could be defined in many different ways. One option is to define each alternative as a broad corridor, without developing the engineering for a specific transportation facility in that corridor. Under this approach, the Tier 1 EIS would compare the alternative corridors based on an inventory of the various resources that are present in each corridor. This approach provides only an approximate basis for comparing the corridors, and may be most appropriate when considering very large study areas. Another option is to develop a "representative alignment" within each corridor considered in the Tier 1 EIS, as a proxy for estimating the likely impacts of building a facility in that corridor. If a representative alignment is developed, some engineering work would be needed, which increases the Tier 1 level of effort but provides a closer approximation of the actual impacts.

- *What environmental information is available at a consistent scale across the study area?*

  The Tier 1 study area often included hundreds (and in some cases, thousands) of square miles, and individual alternatives may be more than one hundred miles long. Environmental data that is available in a high level of detail for some areas may be available at a much lower level of detail in other parts of the study area. To allow for an even-handed comparison of alternatives, it is important to find out what existing environmental data is available on a consistent basis for the entire study area. If there are gaps or inconsistencies, they should be assessed to determine whether additional data-gathering is needed. If the environmental data used has any gaps or inconsistencies, this should be noted in the environmental document in the interest of full disclosure.

- *Are there specific regulatory issues – e.g., Section 4(f) or Section 404 – that must be resolved as part of Tier 1 decision-making?*

In some cases, the choice among Tier 1 alternatives could be governed by legal requirements such as the Section 404 (the "LEDPA" requirement) or Section 4(f). Where this is the case, the Tier 1 EIS will need to include sufficient information to support the analysis required under those laws. For example, FHWA's regulations contemplate that a "preliminary" Section 4(f) evaluation could be included in a Tier 1 EIS. If a preliminary Section 4(f) evaluation is being done, the lead agencies will need to determine *how much* detail is needed to support that evaluation. For example, if there is a large potential historic district that could affect the choice among Tier 1 corridors, it may be necessary to assess the National Register eligibility status of that corridor as part of the Tier 1 EIS.

- *What role will resource agencies have in determining the level of detail?*

If the project is subject to Section 6002 of SAFETEA-LU (23 U.S.C. § 139), the lead agencies must collaborate with the participating agencies in determining "the methodologies to be used and the level of detail required in the analysis of each alternative for a project." (23 U.S.C. § 139(f)(4)(B)). This requirement applies to any EIS initiated for a highway or transit project by FHWA or FTA after August 10, 2005, when SAFETEA-LU was enacted. For a tiered EIS, this means working collaboratively with participating agencies on the core issue of "how much is enough" in the Tier 1 EIS.

- *What actions will be taken to "lock in" the proposed level of detail for Tier 1 studies?*

There is a tendency in any Tier 1 EIS for the level of detail to increase over time, in response to requests from agencies and stakeholders. Changes in approach can strengthen the EIS, but they also can introduce inconsistencies in the way different resources are analyzed. To minimize inconsistencies, and also avoid unnecessary delays, it is good to develop a written work plan that outlines key tasks to be accomplished in Tier 1 and Tier 2. This work plan should identify specific tasks for each resource or topic covered in the EIS – noise, air quality, water quality, community impacts, etc. The work plan can evolve, but it is preferable to have some written plan, including Tier 1 and Tier 2 work, at the outset of the study. For example, the Colorado Department of Transportation developed a comprehensive work plan at the outset of the US 50 tiered EIS. Similarly, the Texas Department of Transportation developed a process manual for the I-69/Trans-Texas Corridor project, which defined the information to be developed and decisions to be made in each tier.

5.2.3 Compliance with Non-NEPA Requirements

Among the greatest challenges in any tiered NEPA process is deciding how to incorporate the consultation, review, and permitting requirements under other laws, including Section 4(f), the National Historic Preservation Act, Endangered Species Act, Clean Water Act, and Clean Air Act. The applicability of these requirements will depend on the specific resources that could be affected by a project, but most large-scale projects will trigger one or more of these laws. Any comprehensive work plan should include careful consideration of these requirements, and should be developed in consultation with agencies that have a direct role in carrying out those laws – for example, the Corps of Engineers for Section 404 permitting.

- *What non-NEPA requirements apply to the project?*

  The first step in developing a strategy for meeting non-NEPA requirements is to determine which laws have the potential to apply to the project. This judgment should be based on existing information and is a starting point for developing a work plan. The goal should simply be to identify a list of the major regulatory issues that may need to be incorporated into the tiered process.

- *How will Section 106 consultation be handled?*

  If the study area includes historic resources, Section 106 consultation will be required at some point during the NEPA process. The key question to decide is whether Section 106 consultation will occur as part of the Tier 1 EIS. If so, it may be advisable to follow a phased approach as allowed under the Section 106 regulations. To help define the framework for the phased approach, the Indiana Department of Transportation developed a Section 106 "work plan" early in the I-69 Tier 1 process, with involvement of the Indiana SHPO and the Advisory Council on Historic Preservation; this work plan was included in the Tier 1 EIS and provided the template for Section 106 consultation in Tier 1 and Tier 2. The Colorado Department of Transportation entered into a Section 106 programmatic agreement in the early stages of the Tier 1 process for the U.S. 50 study; this programmatic agreement also defined the framework for Section 106 consultation in Tier 1 and Tier 2.

- *How will Section 7 consultation be handled?*

  If the study area includes federally listed threatened or endangered species, Section 7 consultation will be required at some point during the NEPA process. Again, the question is whether Section 7 consultation will occur during Tier 1. The lead agencies should consult with USFWS to determine the appropriate timing and structure for Section 7 consultation. One possibility, which was used for the I-69 study in Indiana, is to engage in Section 7 consultation for the entire project during Tier 1, culminating in a Tier 1 Biological Opinion, with follow-on consultation occurring for individual sub-sections during Tier 2 studies. This approach may be most appropriate when endangered species are present along the entire length of the project. If they are more localized, it may be more appropriate to defer Section 7 consultation to Tier 2.

- *How will Section 404 permitting be handled?*

  Most transportation projects involve some impacts to waters of the U.S. and therefore require permitting under Section 404. For a project large enough to involve tiering, the need for a Section 404 permit is a virtual certainty. Early coordination is needed with the Corps of Engineers to resolve a fundamental question: Will a single Section 404 permit be issued for the entire project considered in Tier 1 or will the Corps of Engineers permit each Tier 2 project individually? The answer to this question is important because it will determine the scale at which Section 404 permit decisions – including the LEDPA determination – are made.

- *Is a "NEPA-404 Merger" or similar agreement in place?*

  Several State DOTs have developed procedures for integrating NEPA and Section 404 permitting requirements. These procedures are sometimes documented in agreements that commit federal and state agencies to follow a single "merged" process for completing NEPA and issuing Section 404 permits. Merger agreements generally do not address tiering. Therefore, if a merger agreement is in place, a threshold issue to consider is how to follow the merger process in a Tier 1 study. Will the lead agencies seek concurrence at each of the traditional merger milestones in Tier 1? In particular, will a LEDPA determination be made in Tier 1? If so, can that LEDPA determination be re-opened in Tier 2?

- *How will Clean Air Act conformity be handled?*

For projects in nonattainment or maintenance areas, a project-level conformity determination is needed before NEPA process completion. While the conformity regulations do not address tiering, FHWA has interpreted this requirement to mean that a project-level conformity determination must be made prior to the completion of the Tier 2 study. However, it is prudent for project sponsors to review this issue with the U.S. DOT lead agency and with the EPA to ensure that all parties have a common understanding of how and when conformity requirements will be met.

5.2.4 Technical Tools to Support Tiering

- *What existing data sources will be used to identify environmental resources? Are there significant data gaps that need to be filled?*

Many Tier 1 EISs rely extensively on existing data sources, such as statewide geographic information systems (GIS) mapping libraries, as the basis for identifying environmental resources in the study area. In principle, reliance on existing data sources and GIS mapping is appropriate as part of a tiered EIS (or any EIS). But the quality of the data is an important consideration. If there are significant gaps in the existing data, or if the data for one part of the study area is not comparable to the data available for another area, some additional data-gathering may be needed.

- *What tools will be used to share information with resource agencies?*

Tiered studies often include large study areas, which can make it difficult for resource agency personnel to travel regularly to project meetings or site visits. Web-based tools can be especially valuable for these projects as a way to supplement in-person meetings. These include web-based meetings and secure document-sharing websites. These tools also can be used to enhance communication within the project team.

5.2.5 Educating Agencies and the Public about Tiering

- *What will be done to build support for, and understanding of, the tiered process among resource agencies?*

Resource agencies may be unfamiliar with tiering, or even opposed to tiering, if they believe that it could prematurely commit the transportation agencies to an alternative that would have impacts to sensitive environmental resources. If resource agencies are not willing to support the tiered process, it is unlikely that tiering will be successful. Steps to build resource agency support could include: early coordination, prior to the decision to initiate a tiered study; developing an agency charter or other agreement, outlining mutual commitments in the tiered process; meeting with individual agencies to discuss ways to incorporate their regulatory requirements into the tiered process; providing financial resources to assist agencies in meeting any additional burdens resulting from the tiered process.

- *How will tiering be explained to elected officials, local governments, and the public?*

Many stakeholders will be unfamiliar with tiering and may be concerned that tiering will be used to limit opportunities for them to participate in the process. Building public support for this process will require a sustained effort, not a one-time event. Steps to build stakeholder support for tiering include: visual aids (e.g., flow charts) that explain the major steps in the tiered process; briefings for elected officials, local governments, and community groups; creating a standard description of the tiered process that can be used in all informational materials, briefings, meetings, etc.; communicating with the public through multiple channels, including a website, newsletters, and community meetings.

5.3 Minimizing Litigation Risks

All tiered studies have the potential to encounter a legal challenge, so it is prudent to take steps that will minimize litigation risks. The Indiana I-69 case indicates that courts are willing to accept the use of tiering for large-scale transportation projects, but also shows that courts will rigorously review the lead agency's approach to tiering – not only to evaluate compliance with NEPA, but also to evaluate compliance with other laws. The most significant issues from a legal standpoint may involve compliance with non-NEPA requirements, such as the Endangered Species Act, Clean Water Act, and Section 4(f).

- *Does the EIS explain (a) the reasons for tiering and (b) the basic steps in the tiered process?*

In litigation, courts review agency decisions by considering documents in the administrative record. If tiering is raised as an issue in litigation, courts will look to the administrative record for documents that explain the reasons for tiering and the key steps in the tiered process. This explanation should be included in the Tier 1 EIS. For example, some tiered studies actually include a separate chapter on tiering, which highlights this information. If there are additional documents that explain the tiered process – for example, interagency agreements or work plans), it is helpful to cross-reference those documents in the EIS and perhaps include them as appendices to the EIS.

- *Is there a well-defined approach to meeting each of the non-NEPA requirements? Is it supported by the resource agencies?*

Litigation could challenge tiering not only under NEPA, but also under the other laws that apply to the environmental review process. Lead agencies should systematically identify the legal requirements that apply to the project and determine – for each statute or regulation – how those requirements will be satisfied in the tiered process. The compliance strategy should be documented, showing what actions (if any) will be taken during Tier 1 and what actions will be taken during or after Tier 2. This documentation can be helpful in demonstrating to a court that the agencies involved have considered the relevant legal requirements and have adopted a well-thought-out approach for meeting them.

- *Have any major objections to tiering been raised? How have those objections been addressed?*

The NEPA process provides many opportunities for agencies and the public to submit comments, including any objections they may have to tiering. It is important to document that any major objections to tiering have been considered by the lead agencies and addressed in some manner. Objections can be addressed by modifying the tiered process, or by explaining why the process will not be modified. The key is to show that objections were considered and to respond substantively to those objections.

Tiering can be an effective tool for managing the NEPA process for large-scale and/or complex projects, as well as for preserving a transportation corridor, except where this is prohibited by state law. However, tiering is not an appropriate process for all projects or even all large-scale projects. Prior to initiating a tiered EIS, the reasons for conducting a tiered EIS should be carefully considered to insure that it is the right process for the project. Additionally, because tiering is not regularly used and often requires customization, the process can be confusing to all parties involved. Therefore, early coordination and the development of a partnering agreement with resource agencies and stakeholders, that clearly defines what will be accomplished in Tier 1 and how non-NEPA requirements will be addressed, can be the keys to a successful tiering process.

Appendix A

CEQ Regulations on Tiering

40 C.F.R. § 1502.20 – Tiering
(http://edocket.access.gpo.gov/cfr_2004/julqtr/pdf/40cfr1502.20.pdf)

Agencies are encouraged to tier their environmental impact statements to eliminate repetitive discussions of the same issues and to focus on the actual issues ripe for decision at each level of environmental review (Sec. 1508.28). Whenever a broad environmental impact statement has been prepared (such as a program or policy statement) and a subsequent statement or environmental assessment is then prepared on an action included within the entire program or policy (such as a site specific action) the subsequent statement or environmental assessment need only summarize the issues discussed in the broader statement and incorporate discussions from the broader statement by reference and shall concentrate on the issues specific to the subsequent action. The subsequent document shall state where the earlier document is available. Tiering may also be appropriate for different stages of actions. (Section 1508.28).

40 C.F.R. § 1508.28 – Tiering (http://ecfr.gpoaccess.gov/cgi/t/text/text-idx?c=ecfr&sid=e49159b574ae0a5fb96d9cf8ecb70553&rgn=div8&view=text&node=40:31.0.3.5.9.0.29.28&idno=40)

"Tiering" refers to the coverage of general matters in broader environmental impact statements (such as national program or policy statements) with subsequent narrower statements or environmental analyses (such as regional or basinwide program statements or ultimately site-specific statements) incorporating by reference the general discussions and concentrating solely on the issues specific to the statement subsequently prepared. Tiering is appropriate when the sequence of statements or analyses is:

(a) From a program, plan, or policy environmental impact statement to a program, plan, or policy statement or analysis of lesser scope or to a site-specific statement or analysis.

(b) From an environmental impact statement on a specific action at an early stage (such as need and site selection) to a supplement (which is preferred) or a subsequent statement or analysis at a later stage (such as environmental mitigation). Tiering in such cases is appropriate when it helps the lead agency to focus on the issues which are ripe for decision and exclude from consideration issues already decided or not yet ripe.

Appendix B
CEQ Guidance on Tiering
(All of these documents are available on the CEQ web site at:
http://ceq.hss.doe.gov/nepa/regs/guidance.html)

CEQ, "Forty Most Asked Questions Concerning CEQ's National Environmental Policy Act Regulations" (March 23, 1981) (http://ceq.hss.doe.gov/nepa/regs/guidance.html)

> Tiering is a procedure which allows an agency to avoid duplication of paperwork through the incorporation by reference of the general discussions and relevant specific discussions from an environmental impact statement of broader scope into one of lesser scope or vice versa. In the example given in Question 24b, this would mean that an overview EIS would be prepared for all of the energy activities reasonably foreseeable in a particular geographic area or resulting from a particular development program. This impact statement would be followed by site-specific or project-specific EISs. The tiering process would make each EIS of greater use and meaning to the public as the plan or program develops, without duplication of the analysis prepared for the previous impact statement.

CEQ, "Memorandum for General Counsels, NEPA Liaisons, and Participants in Scoping" (April 30, 1981) (http://ceq.hss.doe.gov/nepa/regs/guidance.html)

> Many people are not familiar with the way environmental impact statements can be "tiered" under the NEPA regulations, so that issues are examined in detail at the stage that decisions on them are being made. See Section 1508.28 of the regulations. For example, if a proposed program is under review, it is possible that site specific actions are not yet proposed. In such a case, these actions are not addressed in the EIS on the program, but are reserved for a later tier of analysis. If tiering is being used, this concept must be made clear at the outset of any scoping meeting, so that participants do not concentrate on issues that are not going to be addressed at this time. If you can specify when these other issues will be addressed it will be easier to convince people to focus on the matters at hand.

CEQ, "Guidance Regarding NEPA Regulations" (1983)
(http://ceq.hss.doe.gov/nepa/regs/guidance.html)

> Tiering of environmental impact statements refers to the process of addressing a broad, general program, policy or proposal in an initial environmental impact statement (EIS), and analyzing a narrower site-specific proposal, related to the initial program, plan or policy in a subsequent EIS. The concept of tiering was promulgated in the 1978 CEQ regulations; the preceding CEQ guidelines had not addressed the concept. The Council's intent in formalizing the tiering concept was to encourage agencies, "to eliminate repetitive discussions and to focus on the actual issues ripe for decisions at each level of environmental review."

> Despite these intentions, the Council perceives that the concept of tiering has caused a certain amount of confusion and uncertainty among individuals involved in the NEPA process. This confusion is by no means universal; indeed, approximately half of those commenting in response to our question about tiering indicated that tiering is effective and should be used more frequently. Approximately one-third of the commentators responded that they had no experience with tiering upon which to base their comments. The remaining commentators were critical of tiering. Some commentators believed that tiering added an additional layer of paperwork to the process and encouraged, rather

than discouraged, duplication. Some commentators thought that the inclusion of tiering in the CEQ regulations added an extra legal requirement to the NEPA process. Other commentators said that an initial EIS could be prepared when issues were too broad to analyze properly for any meaningful consideration. Some commentators believed that the concept was simply not applicable to the types of projects with which they worked; others were concerned about the need to supplement a tiered EIS. Finally, some who responded to our inquiry questioned the courts' acceptance of tiered EISs.

The Council believes that misunderstanding of tiering and its place in the NEPA process is the cause of much of this criticism. Tiering, of course, is by no means the best way to handle all proposals which are subject to NEPA analysis and documentation. The regulations do not require tiering; rather, they authorize its use when an agency determines it is appropriate. It is an option for an agency to use when the nature of the proposal lends itself to tiered EIS(s).

Tiering does not add an additional legal requirement to the NEPA process. An environmental impact statement is required for proposals for legislation and other major Federal actions significantly affecting the quality of the human environment. In the context of NEPA, "major Federal actions" include adoption of official policy, formal plans, and programs as well as approval of specific projects, such as construction activities in a particular location or approval of permits to an outside applicant. Thus, where a Federal agency adopts a formal plan which will be executed throughout a particular region, and later proposes a specific activity to implement that plan in the same region, both actions need to be analyzed under NEPA to determine whether they are major actions which will significantly affect the environment. If the answer is yes in both cases, both actions will be subject to the EIS requirement, whether tiering is used or not. The agency then has one of two alternatives: Either preparation of two environmental impact statements, with the second repeating much of the analysis and information found in the first environmental impact statement, or tiering the two documents. If tiering is utilized, the site-specific EIS contains a summary of the issues discussed in the first statement and the agency will incorporate by reference discussions from the first statement. Thus, the second, or site-specific statement, would focus primarily on the issues relevant to the specific proposal, and would not duplicate material found in the first EIS. It is difficult to understand, given this scenario, how tiering can be criticized for adding an unnecessary layer to the NEPA process; rather, it is intended to streamline the existing process.

The Council agrees with commentators who stated that there are stages in the development of a proposal for a program, plan or policy when the issues are too broad to lend themselves to meaningful analysis in the framework of an EIS. The CEQ regulations specifically define a "proposal" as existing at, "that stage in the development of an action when an agency subject to [NEPA] has a goal and is actively preparing to make a decision on one or more alternative means of accomplishing the goal and the effects can be meaningfully evaluated." Tiering is not intended to force an agency to prepare an EIS before this stage is reached; rather, it is a technique to be used once meaningful analysis can [48 FR 34268] be performed. An EIS is not required before that stage in the development of a proposal, whether tiering is used or not.

The Council also realizes that tiering is not well suited to all agency programs. Again, this is why tiering has been established as an option for the agency to use, as opposed to a requirement.

A supplemental EIS is required when an agency makes substantial changes in the proposed action relevant to environmental concerns, or when there are significant new circumstances or information relevant to environmental concerns bearing on the proposed action, and is optional when an agency otherwise determines to supplement an EIS. The standard for supplementing an EIS is not changed by the use of tiering; there will no doubt be occasions when a supplement is needed, but the use of tiering should reduce the number of those occasions.

Finally, some commentators raised the question of courts' acceptability of tiering. This concern is understandable, given several cases which have reversed agency decisions in regard to a particular programmatic EIS. However, these decisions have never invalidated the concept of tiering, as stated in the CEQ regulations and discussed above. Indeed, the courts recognized the usefulness of the tiering approach in case law before the promulgation of the tiering regulation. Rather, the problems appear when an agency determines not to prepare a site-specific EIS based on the fact that a programmatic EIS was prepared. In this situation, the courts carefully examine the analysis contained in the programmatic EIS. A court may or may not find that the programmatic EIS contains appropriate analysis of impacts and alternatives to meet the adequacy test for the site-specific proposal. A recent decision by the Ninth Circuit Court of Appeals invalidated an attempt by the Forest Service to make a determination regarding wilderness and non-wilderness designations on the basis of a programmatic EIS for this reason. However, it should be stressed that this and other decisions are not a repudiation of the tiering concept. In these instances, in fact, tiering has not been used; rather, the agencies have attempted to rely exclusively on programmatic or "first level" EISs which did not have site-specific information. No court has found that the tiering process as provided for in the CEQ regulations is an improper manner of implementing the NEPA process.

In summary, the Council believes that tiering can be a useful method of reducing paperwork and duplication when used carefully for appropriate types of plans, programs and policies which will later be translated into site-specific projects. Tiering should not be viewed as an additional substantive requirement, but rather a means of accomplishing the NEPA requirements in an efficient manner as possible.

Appendix C
FHWA/FTA Regulations on Tiering

23 C.F.R. § 771.111 – Early Coordination, Public Involvement, and Project Development

(g) For major transportation actions, the tiering of EISs as discussed in the CEQ regulation (40 C.F.R. 1502.20) may be appropriate. The first tier EIS would focus on broad issues such as general location, mode choice, and areawide air quality and land use implications of the major alternatives. The second tier would address site-specific details on project impacts, costs, and mitigation measures.

23 C.F.R. § 774.7 – Documentation

(e) A Section 4(f) approval may involve different levels of detail where the Section 4(f) involvement is addressed in a tiered EIS under §771.111(g) of this chapter.

(1) When the first-tier, broad-scale EIS is prepared, the detailed information necessary to complete the Section 4(f) approval may not be available at that stage in the development of the action. In such cases, the documentation should address the potential impacts that a proposed action will have on Section 4(f) property and whether those impacts could have a bearing on the decision to be made. A preliminary Section 4(f) approval may be made at this time as to whether the impacts resulting from the use of a Section 4(f) property are de minimis or whether there are feasible and prudent avoidance alternatives. This preliminary approval shall include all possible planning to minimize harm to the extent that the level of detail available at the first-tier EIS stage allows. It is recognized that such planning at this stage may be limited to ensuring that opportunities to minimize harm at subsequent stages in the development process have not been precluded by decisions made at the first-tier stage. This preliminary Section 4(f) approval is then incorporated into the first-tier EIS.

(2) The Section 4(f) approval will be finalized in the second-tier study. If no new Section 4(f) use, other than a de minimis impact, is identified in the second-tier study and if all possible planning to minimize harm has occurred, then the second-tier Section 4(f) approval may finalize the preliminary approval by reference to the first-tier documentation. Re-evaluation of the preliminary Section 4(f) approval is only needed to the extent that new or more detailed information available at the second-tier stage raises new Section 4(f) concerns not already considered.

Appendix D
FHWA Memorandum on Tiering
(This document is available at:
http://www.environment.fhwa.dot.gov/guidebook/i70tieringmemo.asp)

Subject: **Information:** <u>Tiering of the I-70 Project</u>   Date: June 18. 2001
<u>Kansas City, Missouri to St. Louis</u>

From: **Original Signed By**   Reply to   HEPE
Frederick Skaer, Director   Attn of:
Office of NEPA Facilitation

To: Allen Masuda, Division Administrator
Jefferson City, Missouri

This is in response to your request for our thoughts on the acceptability and defensibility of relying on the first tier I-70 EIS for establishing logical termini and independent utility for purposes of analysis under the National Environmental Policy Act. Our short answer is that you have broad discretion in how you address these issues in the first and second tier analyses. You should be guided by the desirability of (1) explaining the nature of the first and second tier decision-making so that affected parties are fully aware of their opportunities to influence outcomes at the various decision points and, (2) structuring the decisions to avoid, to the extent possible, a decision on one section forcing an undesirable outcome on another section. Our rationale is explained below.

Our NEPA regulations provide that for major transportation actions the tiering of EISs may be appropriate (23 C.F.R. 771.111 (g)). According to the regulations the first tier would focus on broad issues such as general location, mode choice, and area-wide air quality and land use implications of the major alternatives. The second tier would address site-specific details on project impacts, costs, and mitigation measures. As contemplated in our regulations and in the Council on Environmental Quality regulations, tiering is an option available to organize analysis and decision-making in complex circumstances in a way that takes into account the different geographic scope and timing for different decisions. The difference in scope and timing for the strategic decision of how to address long range needs on a 200 mile long section of I-70 between the major metropolitan areas in Missouri versus the specific location and design decisions for much shorter "projects" on I-70 certainly justifies a tiered approach. Because tiering is an option available to address complex situations, we have deliberately stayed away from prescriptive guidelines on how to apply tiering, so that each tiered process can be custom designed to the specific situation. (The FHWA Technical Advisory 6640.8A, Guidance for Preparing and Processing Environmental and Section 4(f) Documents, does not even mention tiering.) You therefore have considerable latitude in the specific tiering approach you utilize to implement the NEPA policy mandate of informed decision-making.

In exercising your discretion in designing the tiering process, we call your attention to the discussion in the preamble to our NEPA regulation (52 FR 32648; August 28, 1987). The preamble discusses the possibility of using an environmental assessment for second tier actions where no new significant impacts are expected. While not mentioned in the preamble, we could also foresee situations in which minor second tier actions qualified as categorical exclusions.

The same section of the regulation that addresses tiering also contains a provision relating to the geographic scope of actions evaluated in environmental impact statements (EIS) and findings of no significant impact (FONSI) (23 C.F.R. 771.111(f)). This provision specifies a three part test. The actions shall (1) connect logical termini and be of sufficient length to address environmental matters on a broad scope, (2) have independent utility or independent significance, and (3) not restrict consideration of alternatives for other reasonably foreseeable transportation improvements.

Because this three-part test was established with the traditional non-tiered approach to NEPA in mind, we would like to comment on how it should be applied in a tiering situation. As a general rule, we believe that the first part of the test should apply only to the first tier of analysis, i.e. the analysis of sections of sufficient length to address environmental matters on a broad scope is the legitimate purview of the first tier of analysis and decision-making. The second part of the test should be met for both first tier and second tier evaluations since it would not be reasonable to make either strategic decisions or to grant Federal location/design approvals relating to transportation improvements that were not usable and a reasonable public expenditure by themselves. The third part of the test is perhaps the most challenging: we address it below.

The heart of the test's third part is focused on avoiding undesirable outcomes on other reasonably foreseeable transportation improvements, rather than simply preserving the ability to consider alternatives in the abstract. With that in mind, we recommend that you pay specific attention in the first tier of analysis to structuring the decision-making so that the first tier strategic choices made concerning an improvement strategy for I-70 in its entirety not restrict the second tier location and design decisions to alternatives which have highly undesirable consequences, such as unusually severe impacts to communities or the natural environment that might have been avoided with a different first tier strategy.

As you have pointed out, one of the critical first tier tasks is to establish the subsections for second tier analysis. The approach proposed is to present initial thoughts in the first tier DEIS and to solicit comments on appropriate subsections. While maintaining this level of flexibility and openness is admirable and allowable, we suggest that you be somewhat more definite by using the first tier DEIS to identify proposed subsections (rather than initial thoughts) for the second tier analysis. You can maintain flexibility by communicating that the subsections are subject to refinement based on comments received.

The criteria used for establishing subsections should take into account both the purpose and need for the subsection projects, and avoiding "pointing a loaded gun" at an important resource(s) beyond the subsection. For example, subsections being improved primarily because of deteriorated pavement or bridge conditions need not use termini with major changes in traffic volume because the underlying need for the improvement is to address the deteriorated physical condition, not to address the growth in traffic volumes. The same would apply to subsections that are planned for improvement because of localized safety problems. Where the major rationale for improvement concerns congestion and delay, we would envision that the subsections would relate to logical break points in predicted traffic volumes so that the problem is not merely moved to the next section of the highway. To be a logical break point, traffic volumes need not change abruptly; in some cases they would dissipate over a series of interchanges to a point that represented a reasonable end point for a project. Your approach to subdividing the corridor into urban subsections in Columbia, Kansas City, and St. Louis and in intermediate rural subsections is consistent with our thinking. You may even see a benefit to having even smaller tier 2 subsections to address more immediate condition or safety problems.

The tier 1 analysis will give considerable insight into environmental consequences of tier 2 actions. Nevertheless, it is unlikely to provide a detailed understanding of the impacts to many of the resources encountered during the tier 2 analysis. It is therefore important to attempt to locate subsection termini in a way that takes into account what is known from the first tier of analysis but also provides a framework for flexible decision-making at the second tier.

Therefore, we suggest that each of the second tier analyses look beyond the subsection termini to adjacent subsections for which second tier analyses have not yet been undertaken to ensure that one project doesn't point the "loaded gun" at resources associated with the adjacent project. Recent discussions with the Virginia Division indicate that they are drafting an approach to do just that for similar improvements the along the full length of I-81. (In Virginia's case they used a feasibility study rather than a formal NEPA document for the tier 1 analysis, but the difference does not appear to be important to the issues before us). We will ensure that you receive a copy of their approach.

Tiering is by its very nature a complex undertaking. We commend you for taking a lead to look at long-range transportation needs for I-70 from a statewide perspective and thinking about improvements and consequences in a broad based examination. Because you have so much flexibility in customizing the tiering approach to your specific situation, it is critical that you carefully communicate your decision-making process to affected parties. We are available as a sounding board to assist you in this communication. We recommend that you also engage cooperating agencies and others to ensure that your communications are received as intended. One useful mechanism is to employ an editor who has been at arms length from the process to refine the message of the first tier DEIS.

In preparing the above analysis we consulted with Ron Moses of the Chief Counsel's office. If you have any questions about these comments, please contact Lee Dong at 202-366-2054 or Lamar Smith, NEPA Oversight Team Leader, at 202-366-8994.

**Appendix E
Tiered EISs Initiated by FHWA, FTA, and FRA (1999 to 2008)**

Table E-1: Tiered EISs Initiated by FHWA, FTA, and FRA (1999 to 2008)

Project	State	NOI Issued	Mode	Lead	Study Type	Length	Status (as of October 2008)	Studied for this Report / Task 38(Y/N)
Transit Improvements in Beltline Corridor – Atlanta	GA	7/24/2008 73 FR 43278	Transit	FTA	Tier 1	22 miles	Tier 1 in progress. Note: Tier 1 EIS will evaluate and determine transit mode and the general alignment for the transit facility and trails.	N
I-70 – Jackson County – MO/KS State Line to I-470 Interchange (incl. Kansas City Downtown)	MO	7/9/2008 73 FR 39371	Highway	FHWA	Tier 1	18 miles	Tier 1 in progress. Note: Tier 1 EIS will determine Tier 2 sections.	N
State Route 180 Westside Expressway – Fresno County	CA	5/19/2008 73 FR 28854	Highway	Caltrans	Tier 1	20 miles	Tier 1 in progress. Note: FHWA assigned NEPA responsibilities to Caltrans under SAFETEA-LU so Caltrans is the lead agency.	N
I-70 Improvements, Kansas City to St. Louis	MO	4/23/2008 73 FR 22002	Highway	FHWA	Supplement to Tier 1 and 2	200 miles	SEIS in progress. Note: SEIS addresses impacts of dedicated truck lanes.	Y

Guidelines on the Use of Tiered Environmental Impact Statements for Transportation Projects

Table E-1: Tiered EISs Initiated by FHWA, FTA, and FRA (1999 to 2008)

Project	State	NOI Issued	Mode	Lead	Study Type	Length	Status (as of October 2008)	Studied for this Report / Task 38(Y/N)
State Route 25 – San Benito and Santa Clara Counties	CA	4/1/2008 73 FR 17412	Highway	Caltrans	Tier 1	11 miles	Tier 1 in progress. Note: FHWA delegated NEPA responsibilities to Caltrans under SAFETEA-LU so Caltrans is the lead agency.	N
Tappan Zee Bridge/I-287	NY	2/14/2008 73 FR 8740	Highway, Transit	FHWA, FTA	Tier 1	30 miles	Tier 1 EIS in progress. Note: Study began as a non-tiered EIS, with NOI issued on 12/23/2002. Revised NOI issued on 2/14/2008 converted to a tiered EIS.	N
Baton Rouge Loop	LA	2/13/2008 73 FR 8391	Highway (Toll)	FHWA	Tier 1	77 miles	Implementation plan being developed. Not yet in tier 1.	Y
Elgin O'Hare-West Bypass	IL	2/2/2007 72 FR 62293	Highway	FHWA	Tier 1	100 sq miles study area	Tier 1 in progress.	Y
Atlanta to Chattanooga High-Speed Ground Transportation	GA, TN	8/22/2007 72 FR 47121	High-Speed Rail	FHWA, FRA	Tier 1	110 miles	Tier 1 in progress.	Y

Table E-1: Tiered EISs Initiated by FHWA, FTA, and FRA (1999 to 2008)

Project	State	NOI Issued	Mode	Lead	Study Type	Length	Status (as of October 2008)	Studied for this Report / Task 38(Y/N)
SR 11 and Otay Mesa Port of Entry	CA	5/1/2007	Highway	FHWA	Tier 1 (Phased)	3 miles approx.	Tier 1 FEIS issued August 2008	N
California High-Speed Train System – Los Angeles to Orange County	CA	3/15/2007 72 FR 12250	High-Speed Rail	FRA	Tier 2	53 miles	Tier 2 in progress.	Y
California High-Speed Train System – Palmdale to Los Angeles	CA	3/15/2007 72 FR 12252	High-Speed Rail	FRA	Tier 2	58 miles	Tier 2 in progress.	Y
Jacksonville (FL) Rapid Transit System	FL	1/11/2007 72 FR 1364	Transit	FTA	Tier 1 programmatic	35 miles	Tier 1 ROD issued April 2, 2008	N
U.S. 220 from I-68 in MD to Corridor H in WV	WV, MD	4/14/2006 71 FR 19599	Highway	FHWA	Tier 1	42 miles (approx. dependi ng upon corridor)	Tier 1 in progress	N
South Florida East Coast Corridor Transit Analysis	FL	3/28/2006 71 FR 15511	Transit	FTA	Tier 1 programmatic	85 miles	Tier 1 has been complete, but the decision to move forward with tier 2 has not been made	Y

Table E-1: Tiered EISs Initiated by FHWA, FTA, and FRA (1999 to 2008)

Project	State	NOI Issued	Mode	Lead	Study Type	Length	Status (as of October 2008)	Studied for this Report / Task 38(Y/N)
Southeast High Speed Rail – Richmond to Raleigh Section	VA, NC	2/3/2006 71 FR 5903	High-Speed Rail	FRA	Tier 2	138 miles	Tier 2 in progress. Note: This NOI updated the previous NOI for this section, issued in 2003 to change the northern terminus.	Y
U.S. 50 Corridor – Pueblo to Kansas State Line	CO	1/30/2006 71 FR 4958	Highway	FHWA	Tier 1	150 miles	Tier 1 in progress; preparing DEIS.	Y
Lafayette Metropolitan Expressway	LA	12/16/2005 70 FR 74864	Highway (Toll)	FHWA	Tier 1	31 to 38 miles	Tier 1 in progress; preparing DEIS	Y
Bay Area to Central Valley High Speed Train	CA	11/28/2005 70 FR 71370	High-Speed Rail	FRA	Tier 2 programmatic	157 – 360 miles dependi ng upon alternati ve	Tier 1 was completed for entire 700-mile High-Speed Train System; this Tier 2 is also a "programmatic" EIS.	N
Newberg Dundee Bypass	OR	10/14/2005 70 FR 60129	Highway	FHWA	Tier 2	10 miles	Tier 2 in progress. Note: A single Tier 2 EIS will be prepared for full length of Tier 1 project.	Y

Table E-1: Tiered EISs Initiated by FHWA, FTA, and FRA (1999 to 2008)

Project	State	NOI Issued	Mode	Lead	Study Type	Length	Status (as of October 2008)	Studied for this Report / Task 38(Y/N)
I-73 – Hamlet NC to I-95 in SC	SC	7/22/2005 70 FR 42407	Highway	FHWA	Non-Tiered	40 miles	Note: This NOI updated the terminus and converted the study to a non-tiered EIS.	N
I-73 – NC/SC State Line to I-95 in SC	SC	8/9/2004 69 FR 48271	Highway	FHWA	Tier 1	35 miles	Converted to non-tiered EIS.	N
High-Speed Rail Corridor – Las Vegas to Anaheim	CA, NV	5/20/2004 69 FR 29161	High-Speed Rail (Maglev)	FRA	Tier 2 programmatic	269 miles	In progress. Note: Tier 1 involved nationwide programmatic EIS for maglev program.	Y
I-69 Indiana – Section 1 (Evansville to Oakland City)	IN	4/29/2004 69 FR 23618	Highway	FHWA	Tier 2	13 miles	Tier 2 ROD issued.	Y
I-69 Indiana – Section 2 (Oakland City to Washington)	IN	4/29/2004 69 FR 23618	Highway	FHWA	Tier 2	27 miles	Tier 2 in progress	Y
I-69 Indiana – Section 3 (Washington to US 231)	IN	4/29/2004 69 FR 23619	Highway	FHWA	Tier 2	25 miles	Tier 2 in progress.	Y
I-69 Indiana – Section 4 (US 231 to Bloomington)	IN	4/29/2004 69 FR 23620	Highway	FHWA	Tier 2	27 miles	Tier 2 in progress.	Y

Table E-1: Tiered EISs Initiated by FHWA, FTA, and FRA (1999 to 2008)

Project	State	NOI Issued	Mode	Lead	Study Type	Length	Status (as of October 2008)	Studied for this Report / Task 38(Y/N)
I-69 Indiana – Section 5 (Bloomington to Martinsville)	IN	4/29/2004 69 FR 23621	Highway	FHWA	Tier 2	22 miles	Tier 2 in progress.	Y
I-69 Indiana – Section 6 (Martinsville to Indianapolis)	IN	4/29/2004 69 FR 23622	Highway	FHWA	Tier 2	26 miles	Tier 2 in progress.	Y
High-Speed Rail Corridor – Richmond to Hampton Roads	VA	2/23/2004 69 FR 8261	"Higher-Speed" Rail	FRA	Tier 1	100 miles (north corridor) 140 miles south corridor	In progress. Note: This would be an extension of the Southwest High-Speed Rail Corridor.	Y
Trans-Texas Corridor-35 (TTC-35)	TX	2/5/2004 68 FR 5652	Highway, Rail, Transit	FHWA	Tier 1	800 miles	In progress.	Y
I-69/Trans-Texas Corridor	TX	1/15/2004 69 FR 2382	Highway, Rail, Transit	FHWA	Tier 1	1,000	In progress; Tier 1 DEIS issued.	Y

Table E-1: Tiered EISs Initiated by FHWA, FTA, and FRA (1999 to 2008)

Project	State	NOI Issued	Mode	Lead	Study Type	Length	Status (as of October 2008)	Studied for this Report / Task 38(Y/N)
I-81	VA	11/14/2003 68 FR 64674	Highway, Rail	FHWA	Tier 1	325 miles	One of eight identified tier 2 sections is moving forward. Partially being help with up with litigation.	Y
Long Island Railroad – Huntington/Port Jefferson Branch Yard	NY	10/15/2003 68 FR 59441	Commuter Rail	FTA	Tier 2	N/A	Note: This study was tiered from a previous EIS prepared by FTA for the LIRR's East-Side Access project.	N
Placer Parkway Corridor Preservation	CA	11/18/2003 68 FR 54774	Highway	FHWA	Tier 1	15 miles	Note: Tier 1 EIS was prepared to allow corridor preservation.	Y
Trunk Highway 10 (TH-10)	MN	7/28/2003 68 FR 44377	Highway	FHWA	Tier 1	8.4 miles	FHWA terminated EIS on 10/10/2008 (73 FR 60397). Note: Tier 1 EIS was initiated to allow corridor preservation. Tier 2 expected to begin in 10-15 years.	N

Table E-1: Tiered EISs Initiated by FHWA, FTA, and FRA (1999 to 2008)

Project	State	NOI Issued	Mode	Lead	Study Type	Length	Status (as of October 2008)	Studied for this Report / Task 38 (Y/N)
Southeast High Speed Rail Corridor – Petersburg VA to Raleigh NC	VA, NC	5/22/2003 68 FR 28044	High-Speed Rail	FRA	Tier 1	138 miles	Note: Tier 1 ROD was completed for SEHSR corridor from Washington, DC, to Raleigh, NC.	Y
Trunk Highway 41 (TH-41)	MN	1/10/2003 68 FR 1507	Highway	FHWA	Tier 1	3 miles	Note: Tier 1 EIS was prepared to allow corridor preservation. Tier 2 expected to begin in 10-15 years.	Y
Arterial Connecting TH15 and TH 10 (including River Crossing) in St. Cloud, MN	MN	12/26/2002 67 FR 78854	Highway	FHWA	Tier 1	7 miles (approx. depending upon corridor)	Note: Tier 1 EIS was prepared to allow corridor preservation. Tier 2 expected to begin in 15-20 years.	N
I-80, I-29, and I-480 Improvements in Council Bluffs	IA, NE	8/21/2002 67 FR 54256	Highway	FHWA	Tier 1	18 miles	Three of five identified tier 2 sections are proceeding.	Y
M-59 Widening from I-96 to US-23	MI	8/15/2002 67 FR 53384	Highway	FHWA	Tier 2	13 miles	Note: Tier 1 ROD for ROW preservation was signed on 5/31/2002. Single Tier 2 is being prepared for entire length of Tier 1 project.	N

Table E-1: Tiered EISs Initiated by FHWA, FTA, and FRA (1999 to 2008)

Project	State	NOI Issued	Mode	Lead	Study Type	Length	Status (as of October 2008)	Studied for this Report / Task 38(Y/N)
Eastern Corridor (Cincinnati)	OH, KY	6/3/2002 67 FR 38309	Highway, Transit	FHWA	Tier 1	(200 sq. mile study area)	Tier 1 ROD issued. Note: Lawsuit was filed challenging Tier 1 ROD; FHWA decision was upheld.	N
I-70 – Montgomery City to Lake St. Louis	MO	5/10/2002 67 FR 31861	Highway	FHWA	Tier 2	36 miles	Note: Tier 1 ROD was issued in December 2001 for 200-mile I-70 corridor. Note: Tier 1 ROD was issued in December 2001 for 200-mile I-70 corridor. Four EAs and one documented CE have been completed for five of the seven Tier 2 subsections. The Tier 1 ROD was issued in December 2001.	Y
I-70 – Boone County	MO	4/19/2002 67 FR 19469	Highway	FHWA	Tier 2	18 miles		Y

Table E-1: Tiered EISs Initiated by FHWA, FTA, and FRA (1999 to 2008)

Project	State	NOI Issued	Mode	Lead	Study Type	Length	Status (as of October 2008)	Studied for this Report / Task 38(Y/N)
Passenger Rail Improvements – Los Angeles to San Diego	CA	3/20/2002 67 FR 13039	Passenger Rail	FRA	Tier 1 programmatic	150 miles (approx)	Note: This EIS focused on improvements to an existing corridor used by Amtrak and commuter rail; it is separate from the proposed high-speed rail corridor.	N
U.S. 10	WI	9/7/2001 66 FR 46862	Highway	FHWA	Tier 1 and Tier 2	26 miles	Note: A Tier 1 EIS was conducted for the entire corridor for corridor preservation. A Tier 2 EIS was conducted simultaneously for the eastern portion to allow that section to move directly into construction.	Y
Hemet to Corona East-West Transportation Corridor (part of Riverside County Integrated Project)	CA	8/2/2001 66 FR 40312	Highway	FHWA	Tier 1	35 miles (approx. wide corridor still being considered)	Note: The Tier 1 EIS was prepared to allow for ROW preservation.	N

Table E-1: Tiered EISs Initiated by FHWA, FTA, and FRA (1999 to 2008)

Project	State	NOI Issued	Mode	Lead	Study Type	Length	Status (as of October 2008)	Studied for this Report / Task 38(Y/N)
Winchester to Temecula North-South Transportation Corridor (part of Riverside County Integrated Project)	CA	8/2/2001 66 FR 40313	Highway	FHWA	Tier 1	10 miles	Note: The Tier 1 EIS was prepared to allow for ROW preservation.	Y
Baltimore to Washington, DC Maglev Proposal	DC, MD	7/19/2001 66 FR 37721	High-Speed Rail (Maglev)	FRA	Tier 2	38 miles	Note: Tier 1 involved nationwide programmatic EIS for maglev program.	Y
Pennsylvania Maglev Proposal	PA	7/19/2001 66 FR 37721	High-Speed Rail (Maglev)	FRA	Tier 2	54 miles	Note: Tier 1 involved nationwide programmatic EIS for maglev program.	N
California High-Speed Train System	CA	5/2/2001 66 FR 22067	High-Speed Rail	FRA	Tier 1 programmatic	700 miles	Note: This EIS considered routes for the entire 700-mile CA High-Speed Train System.	Y
SR 520 Corridor – Seattle to Redmond	WA	7/18/2000 65 FR 44564	Highway, Transit	FHWA. FTA	Tier 1 programmatic	12 miles	Construction anticipated to begin in 2009.	N

Table E-1: Tiered EISs Initiated by FHWA, FTA, and FRA (1999 to 2008)

Project	State	NOI Issued	Mode	Lead	Study Type	Length	Status (as of October 2008)	Studied for this Report / Task 38(Y/N)
US 301 – Southern Corridor – Prince Georges and Charles Counties	MD	4/12/2000 65 FR 19807	Highway	FHWA	Tier1 / Tier 2	39 miles	Note: Tier 1 level of detail for the majority of the corridor; combined Tier 1/Tier 2 for one portion (the Waldorf area).	Y
I-70 Mountain Corridor	CO	1/25/2000 65 FR 4014	Highway, Rail	FHWA	Tier 1 programmatic	140 miles	Tier 1 in progress; Draft EIS issued. Note: FRA was involved as a cooperating agency. Tier 1 intended to develop 20-year plan and 50-year vision.	Y
I-69 Evansville to Indianapolis (Corridor 18)	IN	1/5/2000 65 FR 551	Highway	FHWA	Tier 1	140 to 170 miles	Tier 1 ROD issued; Tier 2 studies in progress. Note: Lawsuit was filed challenging Tier 1 ROD and Tier 1 Biological Opinion; FHWA and USFWS decisions were upheld.	Y

Guidelines on the Use of Tiered Environmental Impact Statements for Transportation Projects

Table E-1: Tiered EISs Initiated by FHWA, FTA, and FRA (1999 to 2008)

Project	State	NOI Issued	Mode	Lead	Study Type	Length	Status (as of October 2008)	Studied for this Report / Task 38(Y/N)
I-70 Improvements	MO	12/30/1999 64 FR 73599	Highway	FHWA	Tier 1	200 miles	Tier 1 ROD issued; some Tier 2 studies issued; other Tier 2 studies in progress.	Y
Maglev Deployment Program	National	12/29/1999 64 FR 73117	High-Speed Rail (Maglev)	FRA	Tier 1 programmatic	300 (total)	Completed. Tier 2 studies under way for individual projects. Note: Tier 1 was a national EIS that evaluated seven potential Maglev corridors.	N
I-90 Snoqualmie Pass	WA	12/28/1999 64 FR 72717	Highway	FHWA	Tier 1 programmatic	13 miles	FHWA issued a ROD on the FEIS and a preferred alternative has been selected for construction.	N
I-405 Improvements	WA	10/19/1999 64 FR 56380	Highway, Transit	FHWA, FTA	Tier 1 programmatic	30 miles	Tier 1 FEIS issued. Note: Tiered approach was used, but NOI did not describe EIS as tiered.	Y

Table E-1: Tiered EISs Initiated by FHWA, FTA, and FRA (1999 to 2008)

Project	State	NOI Issued	Mode	Lead	Study Type	Length	Status (as of October 2008)	Studied for this Report / Task 38(Y/N)
Southeast High Speed Rail Corridor – Washington, DC to Charlotte NC via Richmond and Raleigh	DC, NC	8/5/1999 64 FR 42753	High-Speed Rail	FHWA. FRA	Tier 1 programmatic	477 miles	Completed. Tier 2 studies under way for individual sections.	Y

Table E-2: Tiered EISs Initiated by FHWA, FTA, and FRA (1999 to 2008)

Tiered EISs Initiated by FHWA, FTA, and FRA (1999 to 2008) Broken down by State

State	Number of Tiered EISs	Number of Tier 1 EISs	Number of Tier 2 EISs	Comments
California	11	8	3	
Colorado	2	2	0	
Georgia	1	1	0	
Florida	2	2	0	
Louisiana	2	2	0	
Illinois	1	1	0	
Indiana	7	1	6	
Maryland	1	1	0	
Michigan	1	0	1	
Minnesota	3	3	0	Includes 1 project that was terminated
Missouri	5	3	2	
New York	2	1	1	One project combined transit and highway
Oregon	1	0	1	
Pennsylvania	1	0	1	
South Carolina	2	2		Both converted to non-tiered
Texas	2	2	0	
Virginia	2	2	0	
Washington	3	3	0	
Wisconsin	1	0	1	
Multi-State (2 states)	9	5	4	
National (>2 states)	1	1	0	
Total	60	40	20	

Appendix F
Task 38 Research Technical Memorandum

Introduction

This appendix presents the research methodology used to compile Project 25-25, Task 38. The research team conducted a literature review to determine the highway and transit projects that were initiated using the tiered environmental process; conducted telephone surveys of department of transportation (DOT), Federal Highway Administration, Federal Transit Administration, and consultants involved in the tiering NEPA process, analyzed this data; and used the data to develop the tiering guidance presented in this report.

Literature Review

The literature review consisted of identifying tiering regulations, guidance, case law, and the Notices of Intent published for tiered linear transportation projects from January 1999 through 2008. This resulted in 60 projects being identified that had initiated the tiered environmental process.

The background materials reviewed included:

- AASHTO's Practitioner's Handbook, "Using the Transportation Planning Process to Support the NEPA Process",

- Council on Environmental Quality (CEQ) Guidance on Programmatic EISs
    - 40 C.F.R. Part 1502.20
    - 40 C.F.R. Part 1508.28
    - CEQ 40 Questions Guidance (1981)
    - CEQ Scoping Guidance (1981)
    - CEQ Memorandum to Federal Agencies (1983)

- William Malley's 2001 Transportation Research Board's (TRB) paper on "Tiered Environmental Studies in the National Environmental Policy Act Process for Highway Projects." [4]

- U.S. Department of Transportation regulations from the Code of Federal Regulations
    - 23 C.F.R. Part 774

- FHWA regulations listed under, 23 CFR 450 and 500, and 49 CFR 613.
    - 23 C.F.R. Part 450
    - 23 C.F.R. Part 500
    - 23 C.F.R. Part 771
    - 49 C.F.R. 613

---

[4] W. G. Malley, A. M. Dusenbury, 2001. *The Use of Tiered Environmental Studies in the National Environmental Policy Act (NEPA) Process for Highway Projects.* Transportation Research Record: Journal of the Transportation Research Board (Volume 1792 / 2002).

- SAFETEA-LU

  - 23 U.S.C. § 139 (Section 6002, SAFETEA-LU, "environmental review process")

- *Hoosier Environmental Council v. USDOT*, 2008 U.S. Dist. LEXIS 90840 (Dec. 10, 2007).

- *Rivers Unlimited v. USDOT.*, 533 F. Supp.2d 1 (D.D.C. 2008)

In both cases the plaintiff's arguments challenging the tiered document were unsuccessful on all counts and summary judgment was awarded to the agencies.

The Federal Register was then searched to identify all notices of intent (NOI) published between January 1999 and October 2008 which announced a project's decision to prepare a tiered EIS document. From this Federal Register search, the research team generated a list of projects to study in more detail.

Interviews

Initial interviews were then conducted with Lamar Smith, Federal Highway Administration Office of Project Development & Environmental Review and Joe Ossi, Federal Transit Administration Office of Planning and Environment, both of whom have extensive experience with tiering. These interviews were conducted to gather input on the study team's approach, to discuss the details which should be identified during the interviews, and to review the list of projects the study team proposed to examine in detail to determine if there were any specific projects they thought the study team should focus on.

From these initial interviews, the survey instrument to be sued during the project interviews was developed to insure key information was consistently gathered from each interview. The survey instrument sought to uncover specific details about why the project's environmental process was conducted as a tiered study, the successes and failures of the tiered study, and the interviewee's perception of tiering, including ideas for improving the process and whether or not they would choose to conduct a tiered study for future projects.

In an effort to gain a complete perspective on what took place during the tiered process, the study team interviewed individuals from the FHWA, FTA, Federal Railroad Administration (FRA), the state departments of transportation (DOTs), consultants, and resource agencies. These interviews were conducted between late August 2008 and November 2008.

From these interviews, project descriptions were developed which are provided in Appendix G. Fifty telephone surveys were conducted that involved 25 of the tiered NEPA projects completed or underway. The interviews were conducted with state DOT, FHWA, FTA, Environmental Protection Agency, and U.S. Corps of Engineers personnel. Interviewees were emailed the Task 38 questionnaire and then a telephone interview was scheduled and conducted. Figure F-1 presents the questionnaire.

Figure F-1

TASK 38 RESEARCH QUESTIONNAIRE

Interviewee: Project:

Interviewer: Date:

Research Plan and Goals

Preparing a tiered EIS for linear transportation projects has become increasingly common in recent years, particularly for lengthy corridors and for projects that involve complex modal decisions. The increasing body of experience with tiering has generated new information about the challenges that practitioners must overcome when preparing a tiered document. This research project presents an opportunity to consolidate the lessons learned from these recent experiences. Key areas of focus for this research project include:

- When to consider a tiered EIS
- What level of detail is appropriate for a Tier 1 vs. Tier 2 EIS
- How to comply with non-NEPA regulatory requirements in a tiered EIS
- Anticipating and addressing potential legal challenges to a tiered EIS
- Technical tools that can support a tiered EIS

Information obtained during the surveys will be used to prepare a synthesis of accumulated results and prepare guidance that consists of:

1. Tiered EISs - What You Need to Know - Part 1 will be a Tiered EIS "101" discussion for environmental professionals who are considering the possibility of a tiered approach but have little or no background or experience with them. The basic mechanics, legal issues, and pros and cons, will be discussed.

2. State of the Practice and Managing Risk - Part 2 will include the findings of the research documented in Subtask 3, including a summary of use nationally over the past eight years (States that have used them and the EISs involved) and the key factors found to be influencing success and failure, including ways to anticipate and manage the risks involved.

3. Does it Apply to this Project? - Part 3 will provide a self-administered, annotated checklist of criteria and issues to consider in determining:

   - whether to prepare a tiered EIS (as compared to a traditional EIS, or a non-NEPA planning study)
   - what level of detail to develop in Tier 1 vs. Tier 2
   - how to comply with non-NEPA regulatory requirements in Tier 1 vs. Tier 2
   - what technical tools to consider for use in Tier 1 vs. Tier 2
   - how to explain key tiering concepts to resource agencies and the public
   - how to minimize risks of a legal challenge to a tiered study

Background

   - What is the current status of the study (Tier 1, Tier 2, etc.)?

   - What is the current status of the project (moving forward, on hold, etc.)?

Figure F-1

- Who were the principal members of the project team (DOT and consultant project managers, primary FHWA contacts)?
- Which people do you suggest contacting? Do you have their contact information?

Approach to Tiering

- When and why was a tiered approach adopted? Who made this decision?
- Did project length play a role in the decision to use tiering?
- What decisions were made in Tier 1 vs. Tier 2?
- What information was developed in Tier 1 vs. Tier 2 (i.e., what level of detail?)
- What alternatives were analyzed in Tier 1 vs. Tier 2?
- What actions were taken to comply with non-NEPA requirements in Tier 1 vs. Tier 2
    - Clean Water Act
    - Endangered Species Act
    - Section 4(f)
    - National Historic Preservation Act
    - Clean Air Act (conformity)
- Did you develop a manual, partnering agreement, or other document outlining the steps that would be taken in each stage of the tiered process? If so, describe what it was and how it was developed. [get a copy of this if available]

Technical Tools

- What technical tools were most useful in carrying out a tiered analysis (e.g., GIS mappings, remote sensing, etc...)?
- Were there tools not at your disposal that would have been helpful during the tiering process? What were they, how could they have helped?

Public and Agency Reactions to Tiering

- What issues / concerns were raised about tiering by the public (cities, special interest groups, elected officials, etc.) and environmental agencies?
- What steps were taken to anticipate and address these concerns? How did you introduce and explain the tiered process to the agencies and the public?
- Did you encounter any major difficulties in obtaining permits or other approvals? Did these difficulties result from use of the tiered process?
    - If so, what issues were raised in the lawsuit?
    - Has the lawsuit been resolved? What was the result?

Figure F-1

Corridor Study vs. Tiering

- o Are you familiar with FHWA / FTA's 2005 guidance on "Linking Planning and NEPA" and February 2007 FHWA-FTA, Appendix A planning regulations?

- o If so ... In the future, would you consider preparing a "corridor study" (pre NEPA) for a lengthy project in lieu of preparing a Tier 1 EIS?

- o What do you see as the pros and cons of preparing a corridor study vs. a tiered NEPA study?

Lessons Learned

- o What, if anything, would have been done differently in hindsight and what advice would be offered to those considering a tiered EIS approach?

    - o How could the process be streamlined?

    - o What was the most difficult part of the tiering process?

    - o To what degree were the anticipated benefits of tiering achieved?

Appendix G
Project Descriptions

Atlanta-Chattanooga High Speed Ground Transportation

Project Summary

The Atlanta-Chattanooga High Speed Ground Transportation study was begun to assess alternatives to highway transportation along the 110-mile corridor between Atlanta, Georgia and Chattanooga, Tennessee. The Georgia Department of Transportation (GDOT) is preparing the Tier 1 EIS. The Federal Railroad Administration (FRA) and FHWA are joint lead agencies under NEPA. The study area is heavily urbanized and consists of numerous rivers and streams. The lead agencies are currently in the process of analyzing project alternatives. Project challenges include managing stakeholder expectations with respect to the timeframe for reaching a decision on the preferred train technology.

Tiering Process

The lead agencies decided to use tiering for the project to allow specific sections of the 110-mile corridor to be studied independently and individual Tier 2 EIS documents to be issued for each section implemented. The available budget, geographic scale and interstate nature of the project played a role in the decision to use tiering. The lead agencies began the Tier 1 study upon publication of the Notice of Intent on August 22, 2007. In Tier 1, the lead agencies are evaluating transportation technologies, assessing general corridor and station locations and selecting a preferred corridor. Some efforts are being taken in Tier 1 to comply with non-NEPA review requirements. A Record of Decision for the Tier 1 EIS is expected to be published in early 2010. In Tier 2, the lead agencies will assess the specific alignments for the entire project and conduct detailed engineering and environmental studies. A separate Tier 2 document will be issued for each section ready for implementation.

Highlights

- FHWA and FRA signed a Memorandum of Agreement to facilitate cooperation during the agencies' evaluation of the use of tiering for the project. Additionally, a coordination plan was developed to ensure compliance with SAFETEA-LU Section 6002.

- The lead agencies engaged in extensive scoping efforts with resource agencies at the beginning of the tiering process to promote coordination.

- Before the NEPA process began, a number of corridor studies were conducted to determine how to address the transportation issues affecting the corridor. The lead agencies are making use of these studies for existing and future conditions analyses.

- The project team has experienced difficulty in managing the expectations of the stakeholders who are providing a portion of the funds for the project. Given the results from many previous (non-NEPA) studies, stakeholders have expressed concerns regarding the length of time needed to reach a decision on a preferred train technology.

Project Website: http://www.fra.dot.gov/us/content/1870

Baton Rouge Loop

Project Summary

The Baton Rouge Loop will be an 80-100 mile highway loop on new alignment around the city of Baton Rouge. The project is being implemented due to Baton Rouge's growing size and increasing traffic congestion.

Tiering Process

The project is currently going through an "implementation plan" which is similar to feasibility study. The NOI for a Tier 1 EIS was published on February 13, 2008. The process has been delayed pending funding availability. The contract to initiate the tiered NEPA process is close to implementation. The primary reason behind doing a Tiered document was the lack of funding available for the NEPA process and to build the road. The tiered process could be used for corridor preservation while funding or arrangements can be made for financing the work.

Highlights

- While the project has not yet entered into the Tiered process, this issue is being resolved as funding is becoming available.

Project Website: http://www.brloop.com/

California High Speed Train System

Project Summary

The California High Speed Train system involves the development of an 800-mile long high speed train system in California providing service between the major metropolitan centers of the San Francisco Bay Area and Sacramento in the north, through the Central Valley, to Los Angeles and San Diego in the south. The California High-Speed Rail Authority (Authority) is the project sponsor and the lead agency for purposes of the California Environmental Quality Act (CEQA) requirements. The Federal Railroad Administration (FRA) is the federal lead agency under NEPA. Possible effects from the project include displacement of properties and conversion of farmland, noise and vibration impacts, impacts to cultural resources, impacts to water resources and wetlands, and impacts to threatened or endangered species habitat.

Tiering Process

Tiering was selected for the project to enable overall analysis of this large-scale proposal and to allow sections of the 800-mile system to be studied independently in Tier 2. The Authority and FRA began the Tier 1 study upon publication of the Notice of Intent on May 2, 2001. A Tier 1 Record of Decision for Program Environmental Impact Report/Environmental Impact Statement (EIR/EIS), a document that complies with both NEPA and CEQA, was published in November 2005. The Authority and FRA prepared a second Tier 1 Program EIR/EIS for the Bay Area to Central Valley section to help identify a preferred corridor alignments and station locations in that area. A Record of Decision for this additional Tier 1 Program EIR/EIS was issued on December 2, 2008. In Tier 1, the agencies assessed high-speed train versus highway and aviation improvements, reviewed corridors, alignments and station options, identified the termini for the individual Tier 2, and identified a preferred high-speed train corridor. Some efforts were taken in Tier 1 to comply with non-NEPA review requirements. Separate Tier 2 documents will be prepared for each section of the project.

Highlights

- Various agreements were executed between the lead agencies and cooperating agencies describing the roles and responsibilities of those involved in the project.

- The FRA entered into a Memorandum of Understanding with cooperating agencies regarding the project's environmental review, and these agencies participated in preparing the Tier 1 EIR/EIS. The lead agencies also engaged in a NEPA/404 merger to minimize the potential for unforeseen issues during the NEPA or Section 404 permitting processes. This led to a concurrence by EPA and the U.S. Army Corps of Engineers that the selected alternative was the Least Environmentally Damaging Practicable Alternative.

- A series of corridor studies were prepared prior to the commencement of the Tier 1 EIR/EIS, which helped to identify the goals for the Tier 1 study.

- The public has had some difficulty understanding the tiering process and the length of time needed to complete the study.

Project Website: http://www.cahighspeedrail.ca.gov/eir_final/Default.asp
http://www.fra.dot.gov/us/content/1187

Council Bluffs Interstate System Improvements

Project Summary

The Council Bluffs Interstate System Improvements project was initiated to enhance mobility throughout the I-80, I-29, and I-480 corridors within the Council Bluffs metropolitan area in Iowa. The project is comprised of approximately 18 miles of mainline interstate improvements and 14 interchanges, three of which are system (interstate-to-interstate) interchanges. The Iowa Department of Transportation (Iowa DOT) is sponsoring the project. FHWA is the lead agency under NEPA. Potential effects of the project include impacts to the Missouri River and residential/commercial properties.

Tiering Process

Iowa DOT, in conjunction with the FHWA, decided to use tiering for the project because of the size and complexity of the urban interstate system and the multi-project approach to the improvements. The estimated cost of the project and the duration to develop and construct the projects played a role in the decision to use tiering. The agencies began the Tier 1 study upon publication of the Notice of Intent on August 21, 2002. The Tier 1 EIS was signed in July 2005 and a Record of Decision for the Tier 1 EIS was published shortly thereafter. The Tier 1 EIS analyzed highway and transit alternatives for the interstate system improvements and selected a preferred system alternative. The Tier 1 EIS also identified the termini for the individual Tier 2 sections. The Tier 1 study deferred compliance with specific non-NEPA requirements until Tier 2. Separate Tier 2 documents have been approved for two of the five Tier 2 sections. Construction on Segment 1 began in 2008. Construction on Segments 2 and 3 is expected to begin in 2012.

Highlights

- In 1997, prior to initiating the NEPA process, the city of Council Bluffs and the Metropolitan Area Planning Agency conducted the Council Bluffs Interstate System Needs Study. The Needs Study provided a starting point for the tiered NEPA study.

- In Tier 1, the Iowa DOT engaged in the NEPA/404 Merger Concurrence Process, required in Iowa, to gain early input from the resource agencies on the project. The resource agencies were reluctant to concur in this process because of the lack of detail given to environmental impacts in Tier 1.

- The lack of a partnership agreement or other plan for how the tiering process would be used caused some delays in the project, as the Iowa DOT and FHWA had to slow project development at times to reevaluate the process.

- Tiering improved and quickened the Tier 2 process, as well as final design and construction.

Project Website: http://www.cbinterstate.com/default.asp
http://www.fhwa.dot.gov/construction/accelerated/wsia0602.cfm

Elgin O'Hare West Bypass

Project Summary

The Elgin O'Hare West Bypass study is evaluating transportation needs and system alternatives within the area surrounding O'Hare International Airport and northwest of the airport within Cook and DuPage Counties near Chicago, Illinois. The Illinois Department of Transportation (IDOT) is sponsoring the project, and IDOT and FHWA are acting as joint lead agencies for the NEPA study. The study area includes approximately 127 square miles of densely developed residential, commercial, and industrial lands with approximately 52 miles of streams, nearly 8,000 acres of floodplains, more than 2,700 acres of wetlands, and more than 1,200 acres of threatened and endangered species habitat. The O'Hare airport expansion, a separate project, has travel demand and design implications for any adjacent roadway improvements, and has been a historical source of disagreement amongst surrounding communities.

Tiering Process

The agencies jointly decided to use tiering for this project to facilitate the selection of a single multi modal transportation system for a large study area with complex transportation issues and no known solution. IDOT and FHWA began the Tier 1 study upon publication of the Notice of Intent on November 2, 2007. In Tier 1, the lead agencies are studying roadway and transit alternatives. The Tier 1 EIS will examine multiple corridors and roadway/transit network alternatives that will eventually form the basis for a preferred transportation system alternative for the study area. A Record of Decision for the Tier 1 EIS is anticipated in October 2010. In Tier 2, detailed engineering and environmental studies will be conducted for the individual project corridors that comprise the selected alternative and have operational independence. Separate Tier 2 EIS documents will be issued for the individual project corridors identified in the Tier 1 EIS.

Highlights

- IDOT and FHWA engaged in lengthy discussions to weigh the benefits and drawbacks of using tiering for this project. Once the agencies determined that tiering was appropriate, they prepared a document outlining how they would proceed.

- At the beginning of the tiered process, IDOT prepared a stakeholder involvement plan to provide the framework for achieving consensus and communicating the decision-making process to stakeholders. In addition, to build community consensus and promote involvement, IDOT employed the Context Sensitive Solutions process, an inter-disciplinary approach to project development that focuses on stakeholder involvement.

- IDOT and FHWA engaged in extensive public education activities comprised of public meetings, newsletters and press releases, and a regularly-updated project website.

- The lead agencies are utilizing the Illinois NEPA/404 merger process to involve resource agencies early in the development of the project and minimize the potential for unforeseen issues.

Project Website: http://www.elginohare-westbypass.org

Highway 41 (Carver and Scott Counties, MN)

Project Summary

A new bridge crossing the Minnesota River is being proposed as a four-lane highway providing a freeway to freeway connection of US Highway 169 and new US 212 in the vicinity of TH 41 with a total project length of between 3.0 – 3.9 miles. The Minnesota Department of Transportation (MnDOT) is the lead agency for the project, with the Federal Highway Administration (FHWA) being the lead federal agency. The project is being undertaken to accommodate anticipated growth and relieve congestion, noise, and vibration in the area of a historic district in downtown Chaska. Although funding for construction is not currently included in either the MnDOT's or the Metropolitan Council's (local MPO for the Twin-Cities) 20-year transportation plans, there is budget for the purchase of right-of-way (ROW).

Tiering Process

The NOI for this project was released on January 10, 2003. The project is being undertaken as a tiered project to identify a 300-foot wide corridor and preserve ROW in the near term as the study area is rapidly developing, and also because funding for construction is not within current plans. A Tier 1 DEIS which studied six alternative locations was approved on June 4th, 2007. The six alternatives examine various ways to connect US Highway 169 with new US Highway 212 while avoiding historic Chaska and elevating the roadway above the floodplain. Each of the alternatives considered the development of a four-land highway. Currently the project team is continuing consultations with stakeholders to build consensus towards a preferred alternative with an FEIS anticipated in the Spring of 2009 and a record of decision (ROD) in the Summer of 2009.

Highlights

- Two committees were formed to help facilitate the project: The Study Advisory Committee meets bi-monthly to provide information, review technical work, and comment on the study, and The Policy Advisory Committee which reviews findings at key points in the study and to provide input regarding how the study relates to regional and local government concerns.

- A previous DEIS was completed in the 1980's, which identified a corridor through a highest quality wetland. The associated counties and cities preserved the ROW for this corridor and want it to be considered as an alternative.

- There is the question as to whether funding will be available to purchase ROW once the corridor is identified, so MnDOT and FHWA may need to depend upon local municipalities and cities to preserve the corridor ROW until the state has the funding to purchase it.

- As part of Tier 1, a §106 Programmatic Agreement was developed, a §404 letter of concurrence was received, and §4f evaluation was completed.

Project Website: http://projects.dot.state.mn.us/srf/041/

I-69/Trans-Texas Corridor

Project Summary

The I-69/Trans-Texas Corridor (I-69/TTC) project is part of a planned 1,600 mile national highway (I-69) serving the U.S. between the borders of Mexico and Canada. In 2002, the Texas Department of Transportation (TxDOT) integrated I-69 in Texas with its Trans Texas Corridor (TTC) System Plan, a state initiative for accommodating Texas' growing transportation needs. The I-69/TTC Tier 1 Environmental Impact Statement (EIS) study area is 650 miles long and 20 to 80 miles wide from Texarkana, TX and Shreveport, LA to Laredo, TX and the Rio Grande Valley. The I-69/TTC would provide for a multi-modal transportation system with interstate highway, exclusive truck lanes, freight and passenger rail lines, and space for future utility use.

Tiering Process

TxDOT and FHWA elected to use the Tiered NEPA approach, publishing the NOI for a Tier 1 EIS on January 15, 2004. Because I-69/TTC is in the early planning stages, has a 50 year project planning horizon, and is large and complex in scope, a tiered NEPA approach was chosen. The Tier 1 DEIS was released for public review on November 9, 2007. The alternatives considered in Tier 1 were the no action, use of existing/planned transportation facilities, and new location corridor alternatives ranging between one half to four miles wide. These alternatives were going to be carried forward into a Tier 2 analysis, so they were not analyzed. The Tier 1 DEIS recommended that a new location corridor as well as the existing/planned transportation facilities alternative be advanced as the study area for Tier 2 in which alignment level alternatives would be developed and evaluated, as needed.

Highlights

- Funding has been the primary reason for delaying this project. A comment was made that if the finances are not available to conduct the entire study, the necessity of tiering and the anticipated outcomes should be carefully examined prior to starting.

- A process manual was developed which established concurrence points at key project milestones, and a process to promote collaborative decision-making.

- TxDOT and the FHWA created a Technical Advisory Committee to participate in the decision making process, and a Steering Committee which was responsible for policy level oversight in addition to participating in the project decision-making process.

- 11 public scoping meetings, 37 public information meetings, and 47 public hearings were conducted throughout the study area, but the general consensus remained that the public had difficulty understanding the tiering process.

- The resource agencies felt that putting more time into Tier 1, defining ways to minimize impacts or to implement best management practices, would have allowed them to follow a more streamlined approach for approving Tier 2 projects and issuing permits.

- The resource agencies felt they would have a difficult time signing off on a ROD when there had not been an assessment of impacts for the alternatives.

Project Website: http://ttc.keeptexasmoving.com/projects/i69/

I-69 Evansville to Indianapolis

Project Summary

The I-69 Evansville to Indianapolis project involves the construction of an Interstate highway connecting Evansville to Indianapolis, Indiana – a distance of approximately 140 miles. The study area encompassed a land area of about 10,000 square miles. The Indiana Department of Transportation (INDOT), the project sponsor, has been planning an Evansville to Indianapolis highway for more than 50 years, but the project had not been implemented for financial and other reasons. In the 1990s, Congress designated I-69 as a national "high priority corridor" connecting Canada to Mexico. Based on this legislation, INDOT, along with the FHWA, the lead agency under NEPA, initiated a NEPA study for the project. Potential environmental effects of the project include impacts to Indiana bat and bald eagle habitat, environmentally sensitive karst areas (caves, springs and sinkholes), farmland and historic properties.

Tiering Process

INDOT and FHWA prepared a tiered NEPA study because of the geographic scale of the project and the size of the study area. The agencies began the Tier 1 study upon publication of the Notice of Intent on January 12, 2000. A Record of Decision for the Tier 1 EIS was published in March 2004. The Tier 1 EIS analyzed alternatives and selected a preferred corridor which is generally 2,000 feet in width. The Tier 1 EIS also identified the termini for the individual Tier 2 sections. Extensive efforts were taken in Tier 1 to satisfy non-NEPA review requirements, resulting in a Tier 1 Biological Opinion, air quality conformity, and other environmental documents. Six separate Tier 2 studies were initiated in March 2004 to select the specific alignment, interchange locations and design characteristics of each section and to develop more detailed mitigation measures. A Record of Decision for the Section 1 Tier 2 EIS was approved in December 2007, and Section 1 is currently under construction.

Highlights

- INDOT and FHWA engaged in extensive correspondence with resource agencies in deciding to use tiering and throughout the development of the project. This coordination determined the appropriate level of analysis for individual resources in the Tier 1 study.

- As a result of Indiana bat and bald eagle habitat along the preferred corridor, Tier 1 involved a more detailed analysis of Endangered Species Act considerations than Tier 1 studies typically involve.

- INDOT has used a consistent approach for the NEPA documentation in each Tier 2 section by using the Section 1 EIS as a template. This promotes a uniform format, conformity with resource agency expectations, and time and costs savings.

- The project has seen substantial opposition. Several environmental groups filed a lawsuit against FHWA and the U.S. Fish and Wildlife Service (USFWS) based on the Tier 1 EIS, challenging FHWA's decisions under NEPA and Section 4(f) and the USFWS's Biological Opinion. The lawsuit was decided in favor of the agencies, and no appeal was taken.

Project Website: http://www.i69indyevn.org/

I-70 Improvements Missouri

Project Summary

The project is to improve I-70 across the entire state of Missouri, from St. Louis to Kansas City. The study area was 199 miles long and 10 miles wide, including five miles north and five miles south of I-70. The project was undertaken to replace an old pavement structure, increase capacity, improve the efficiency of freight movements, and to increase traffic safety.

Tiering Process

The NOI to conduct a Tier 1 EIS for the improvements to I-70 in Missouri was published on December 30, 1999. The Tier 1 DEIS was published in September 2001, and the FEIS and ROD were both received in December 2001. It was determined that tiering would be used prior to the start of the project because of the project length. Tiering was originally proposed by MoDOT and was met with resistance by the FHWA because of unsuccessful attempts in completing Tiered EIS projects around the nation.

Tier 1 focused on what strategy the project team was going to utilize for improving I-70. Tier 1 originally considered developing the project on entirely new alignment or widening the existing alignment, with the decision made to widen I-70 at its existing location to a minimum of six lanes across the state. The resource agencies participated in the entire process, and were comfortable with the process. From the start, everyone understood that level of detail would be much less than what they were used to seeing in a traditional EIS, and that if any potential major impact was found in Tier 2, the impact would be dealt with in the Tier 2 studies. Additionally seven sections of independent utility were identified in Tier 1. Tier 2 studies consisted of five EISs, one EA, and one documented CE and were successfully completed.

Highlights

- Consultation with all parties prior to starting the tiering process, insured that everyone understood what was expected out of each tier.

- Bringing all of the parties together in one setting allowed all of the agencies to voice their concerns in front of the entire group. Each agency was able to hear the concerns of the other agencies and how their concerns were going to be addressed. This led to a collaborative process and built strong working relationships.

- Tiering allowed all major corridor issues to be addressed at once providing a decisional point with minimal effort, thereby streamlining Tier 2.

- The lack of available funding caused delays in the project

- The MPOs in St. Louis and Kansas City were not initially fully engaged in the project, but later the project team felt there should have been greater MPO involvement which would have greatly enhanced the process.

- The ACOE provided conditional permits in Tier 1 based upon information as it became available.

Project Website: http://www.improvei70.org/4_technical_main.html

I-70 Mountain Corridor

Project Summary

The I-70 Mountain Corridor project was implemented to take a broad view of the transportation issues and alternative solutions for improvements to the 144-mile I-70 mountain corridor from the intersection of I-70 and C-470 to Glenwood Springs. The Colorado Department of Transportation (CDOT) is sponsoring the project and is preparing the Tier 1 EIS for the FHWA, the lead agency under NEPA. Potential impacts of the project include wildlife habitat and migration patterns, historic properties, and wetlands. Project challenges include delays in reaching an agreement on a preferred alternative and managing the expectations of the public and resource agencies.

Tiering Process

CDOT, in coordination with the FHWA, decided to use tiering for the project due to the geographic scale of the project, the complexity of the corridor, the multi-jurisdictional nature of the corridor, and the time needed for project development and construction. The agencies began the Tier 1 study upon publication of the Notice of Intent on January 25, 2000. In Tier 1, the agencies are analyzing highway and transit alternatives for the corridor and identifying a preferred alternative. Extensive efforts are being taken in Tier 1 to comply with non-NEPA review requirements. A Tier 1 draft EIS was prepared in November 2004 and a Record of Decision for a Tier 1 final EIS is expected to be published in 2010. In Tier 2, the agencies will develop separate Tier 2 documents for specific corridor improvements.

Highlights

- More than 30 political jurisdictions formed the I-70 Coalition by adopting an intergovernmental agreement to promote coordination.

- The project involves a "Collaborative Effort," convened by CDOT to facilitate discussion among local governments, highway users, environmental groups, and agencies.

- To build community consensus and promote involvement throughout the study process, the agencies employed the Context Sensitive Solutions (CSS) process, an inter-disciplinary approach to project development that focuses on stakeholder involvement. A corridor-wide guidance manual for decision-making in Tier 2 is currently being developed by the CSS team, as are a historic context report and civic design guidelines.

- Before the NEPA process began, a feasibility study and a Major Investment Study were completed to identify short- and long-term mobility solutions within the corridor. These studies provided a starting point for the development of alternatives in the Tier 1 EIS, but nonetheless, much of the work had to be reevaluated during the Tier 1 study.

- Tier 1 has involved a greater degree of environmental detail than is typically included in Tier 1 due to the intensity of the environmental issues and the public's concerns. A number of Memoranda of Understanding have been developed to address various issues.

Project Website: http://www.dot.state.co.us/I70mtncorridor/

I-81 Corridor Improvement Study

Project Summary

The I-81 Corridor Improvement Study was initiated to analyze safety and operational improvements and address concerns regarding the future capacity of the 325-mile I-81 corridor spanning the Commonwealth of Virginia from approximately Winchester to Bristol. The Virginia Department of Transportation (VDOT) and FHWA, the lead federal agency under NEPA, are co-sponsoring the project and jointly completing the NEPA study. Potential impacts of the project include agricultural lands, historic properties and archaeological sites, and parks and recreation areas.

Tiering Process

VDOT and FHWA decided to use tiering for the project to streamline the environmental study of the corridor by dividing the study into two phases. The geographic scale of the corridor played a role in the decision to use tiering. The agencies began the Tier 1 study upon publication of the Notice of Intent on November 14, 2003. A Record of Decision for the Tier 1 EIS was published in June 2007. The Tier 1 EIS analyzed highway and rail alternatives for the corridor and selected a preferred alternative. The Tier 1 EIS also identified the termini for the individual Tier 2 sections. Some efforts were taken in Tier 1 to comply with non-NEPA review requirements. In Tier 2, the agencies are conducting separate studies for each section to assess independent highway and rail components. The Tier 2 studies will include an I-81 Freight Rail Study being conducted by the Virginia Department of Rail and Public Transportation, in cooperation with Norfolk Southern Railway, to identify specific short-term rail improvement projects in Virginia. A Tier 2 document is underway for one of eight sections of the project.

Highlights

- VDOT and the FHWA prepared a Process Streamlining Agreement at the beginning of the tiered process to define the decisions to be made and approvals to be granted throughout the study and to define the process and elements of each tier. The agreement has been instrumental to the success of the study.

- VDOT included a chapter on tiering in the Tier 1 EIS which discussed the tiering process, the regulatory framework behind tiering, and the Process Streamlining Agreement between VDOT and FHWA. This helped the public to understand the process.

- Due to limited funding, VDOT is currently pursuing a Tier 2 study for only one of the eight project sections.

- The public had some difficulty understanding the tiered process and expected more detailed environmental analyses in Tier 1 than typically included.

Project Website: http://www.i-81.org/ http://www.vdot.virginia.gov/projects/constSTAN-I-81-environment.asp

I-405 Corridor Program

Project Summary

The I-405 Corridor Program involves a tiered NEPA study that outlines transit, roadway, and environmental investments to the 30-mile I-405 corridor in the Puget Sound region of Washington State. The project includes more than 150 coordinated projects to relieve congestion along the corridor, including adding two lanes to I-405, incorporating a corridor-wide bus rapid transit line and building new park-and-ride spaces. The project is jointly sponsored by the Washington Department of Transportation (WSDOT) and FHWA. The co-lead agencies for the NEPA study are WSDOT, FHWA, the Federal Transit Administration (FTA), the Central Puget Sound Regional Transit Authority, and the King County Department of Transportation. Potential environmental effects of the project include impacts to air quality, water quality, and endangered Chinook salmon habitat.

Tiering Process

WSDOT, with involvement from FHWA, decided to use tiering to establish a multi-modal transportation vision for the corridor. The lack of funding for the corridor improvement projects also played a role in the decision to use tiering. The complexity of the 30-mile corridor also played a role in the decision to use tiering. The agencies began the Tier 1 study upon publication of the Notice of Intent on October 4, 1999. A Record of Decision for the Tier 1 EIS was published in October 2002. The Tier 1 EIS assessed highway and transit alternatives and identified a preferred alternative for corridor improvements. Some efforts were taken in Tier 1 to comply with non-NEPA review requirements. The Tier 1 EIS identified specific Tier 2 projects. Tier 2 studies are being performed for the more than 150 individual projects in the corridor. Eleven Tier 2 studies are currently underway, and a number of projects are under construction.

Highlights

- The Tier 1 EIS was a "NEPA reinvention" pilot project, which at the time was a new approach for gaining public and regulatory agency involvement in the decision-making process. The approach was developed by FHWA and WSDOT.

- The lead agencies encountered minor difficulties in gaining the approval of the resource agencies on the analyses performed in Tier 1. The resource agencies expected a more detailed level of analysis than what could be accommodated in a typical Tier 1 EIS.

- WSDOT has used a consistent approach for each Tier 2 project along the I-405 corridor by providing outlines and methodologies for completed projects to the consultants for subsequent projects, thereby promoting a uniform format for Tier 2 studies as well as time and costs savings. Additionally, WSDOT has streamlined the process by using the same consulting firms for different Tier 2 projects.

- By using tiering, WSDOT has been able to obtain approval for individual construction projects along the I-405 corridor independently of other Tier 2 projects. Difficulties encountered with one project do not affect the other projects.

Project Website: http://www.wsdot.wa.gov/Projects/i405

Lafayette Metro Expressway

Project Summary

The proposed project, the Lafayette Regional Expressway (LRX) is a proposed facility to be built on new alignment near the Lafayette, Louisiana region to enhance regional and national transportation and alleviate congestion on local arterial roads and streets. The LRX is proposed as a controlled access toll road using new location to connect I-49 north of Lafayette, I-10 west of Lafayette, and US 90 south of the city of Lafayette.

Tiering Process

The project was tiered from the beginning primarily because there was not enough money to do a traditional NEPA document for the entire project. Project size and expense were both primary considerations in the determination to follow the tiered process. The NOI was published on December 16, 2005, and to date there is still no environmental document ready for publication. Tier 1 will examine five corridor alternatives for the loop facility and examine the potential impacts of each at a high level. Tier 2 will identify a preferred alternative alignment and facility design within the LRX corridor.

Highlights

- Funding has been the major issue with delaying this project. A comment was made that if the finances are not available to conduct the entire study, the need for starting a tiered process and the anticipated outcomes should be carefully examined.

- A major issue has been identifying properties within the Tier 1 corridors which may be taken. This puts those property owners on notice, many of whom have responded that they feel their lives are now on hold until it is decided where and when this project will be built.

- Local communities that will be impacted are attempting to develop zoning codes that will preserve the corridor and enhance the values of the properties along the corridor.

Project Website: http://www.lafayettexpressway.com/

Las Vegas – Anaheim High Speed Rail
(California-Nevada Interstate Maglev Project)

Project Summary

The project is a 269 mile Maglev line corridor running between Las Vegas and Anaheim that was originally part of the Federal Rail Administration's (FRA) Maglev Development Program. The first 40 eastern most miles, from Las Vegas to Primm, Nevada and the new airport being developed there is planned to be a demonstration of Maglev technology. The Maglev train, reaching speeds of 300 mph can make the 24 mile trip from Primm to Las Vegas in eight minutes. The project is currently on hold until matching funds become available.

Tiering Process

The NOI for this project released on May 20, 2004, announced that the project was going to be tiered as part of a decision by the FRA as part of the national Maglev program. The project team, led by the Nevada DOT and the FRA utilized the original fatal flaw Maglev studies as the basis for the Tier 1 studies. The initial intent was to go through the Tier 1 process for the entire corridor and simultaneously conduct Tier 2 studies for the first 40 eastern most miles from Primm to Las Vegas. Tier 1 was intended to identify a preferred corridor and the potential impacts for each of these corridors which would be further studied in Tier 2.

Highlights

- This was the first tiered project worked on by the Nevada DOT

- Lack of funding has prevented the project team from fully engaging in the process.

- Slow progress on the project, due to lack of funding, has caused some of the previously identified corridors to be modified to adapt to development in the Las Vegas area.

- Project team wanted to develop as much work as possible in Tier 1 to streamline Tier 2.

- An MOU was developed between the FRA, Nevada DOT, California/Nevada Super Speed Train Commission, and CalTrans prior to initiating the NEPA process. This focused on the administration of the NEPA/CEQA process.

- Developed an Agency Advisory Committee to actively engage the resource agencies early and often. Key to the success was getting all the parties together early to coordinate roles and responsibilities.

- A detailed scope of work was prepared for participating parties that identified project steps and a scope of work.

- Biggest point of frustration was the on-again / off-again nature of the project from the federal level with funding coming in small increments.

- It is essential that all parties understand what a Tier 1 is supposed to do and the reality of the cost to them, including what level of analysis is required.

Project Website: http://www.fra.dot.gov/us/content/1473

Maglev – Baltimore to Washington D.C.

Project Summary

The 40 mile long high speed corridor links downtown Baltimore and the Baltimore-Washington International Airport with Washington D.C. The project was advanced as part of the Federal Railroad Administration's (FRA) Maglev Deployment Program under TEA-21. The first Tier for this project was a Draft and Final Programmatic EIS and ROD that evaluated building a maglev system in numerous locations, treated as EIS alternatives, throughout the U.S. The NOI to prepare a site specific Tier 2 document for the Baltimore to Washington DC project was published in July 2001. The Maryland Transit Administration (MTA), as the local lead agency, developed the environmental documentation with oversight from the FRA. Currently, the project has submitted a Draft FEIS which includes responses to public hearing comments, updates to the DEIS, and more detailed   no-build alternative descriptions. The project is on hold for additional funding to complete the environmental documentation and reach a ROD on the Tier 2 EIS.

Tiering Process

The project was tiered as part of FRA's decision-making tool for the nationwide program, not because of the project length or size. A Programmatic EIS examined seven locations for first maglev project in the U.S., including the Baltimore- Washington 'alternative'. The NOI for this EIS was released on July 19, 2001. As part of the site-specific EIS for the Baltimore to Washington project, pre-permitting coordination with the resource agencies has been conducted, laying the foundation for advancing permits. Various alignments were also considered, with the MTA recommending that the alternative paralleling the current Amtrak line be retained for a more detailed study. Also, as a result of the PEIS, the Pittsburgh, Pennsylvania 'alternative' was selected and funded to prepare a Tier 2 EIS. The Baltimore-Washington Maglev project released the DEIS in October 2003.

Highlights

- A budget finance resolution limited funding to a million dollars which limited what could be done.

- The project team used adaptive environmental management, adding two steps to the traditional environmental model: predict, mitigate, implement, monitor, and adapt.

- Proposed that under Tier 2, Memoranda of Agreement would be developed on the key environmental issues with specific resource agencies.

- A national initiative for Maglev rail would help push this project forward significantly

- Continuity of agency and project staff, keeping the project moving forward, and keeping the public's attention are all key in a successful tiered project.

- By tiering the NEPA documents, the FRA was able to use the findings of the PEIS to determine recommended locations or alternatives for the site specific Tier 2 EISs

Project Website: http://www.bwmaglev.com/

Newberg Dundee Bypass

Project Summary

The Newberg Dundee Bypass Project (Bypass) was implemented as part of the Newberg Dundee Transportation Improvement Project (NDTIP), which seeks to improve regional and local transportation along the Oregon Highway 99W corridor in the Newberg and Dundee area in Yamhill County, Oregon. The Oregon Department of Transportation (ODOT) led the preparation of the Tier 1 EIS in coordination with the FHWA, who is the lead agency for the NEPA study. The Bypass corridor is approximately 11 miles long from the Oregon 99W/Oregon 18 intersection to the Rex Hill area east of Newberg at Oregon 99W mile post 20.08. Potential project impacts include wetlands and farmland. Project challenges include a lack of funding for both the study and construction and stringent land-use planning obligations required by the State of Oregon.

Tiering Process

ODOT decided to use tiering for the NDTIP in 2000 in an effort to streamline the project and minimize the land-use planning effort required by the State of Oregon. ODOT began the Tier 1 study upon publication of the Notice of Intent on October 14, 2005. A Record of Decision for the Tier 1 EIS was published in August 2005. The Tier 1 EIS identified alternative corridors for the Bypass and selected a corridor that is at least 330 feet wide and reaches or exceeds 400 feet in width at some points. The Tier 1 study involved a broad overview of environmental issues, but deferred compliance with specific non-NEPA requirements until Tier 2. The Tier 2 EIS, currently in progress, involves aligning the Bypass within the preferred corridor, identifying interchanges and local road circulation, and evaluating detailed engineering options. A draft Tier 2 EIS is expected to be published in late spring 2009 and a Record of Decision issued in late 2010.

Highlights

- ODOT did not find tiering to be the best process for this project. State-required land-use planning efforts were required regardless of the NEPA process used, and therefore, tiering did not help to relieve these pressures or streamline the process.

- ODOT entered into agreements with various units of local government in which the parties made a statement of good faith about the expected accomplishments of the project and the anticipated actions that would be necessary to comply with state land-use planning requirements. These agreements facilitated cooperation.

- ODOT entered into an agreement with the resource agencies to outline ODOT's commitments for the Tier 2 EIS. The resource agencies' concurrence with the preferred corridor was contingent upon ODOT's future accomplishment of these commitments.

- A series of corridor studies were prepared prior to the commencement of the Tier 1 EIS, which helped to define the goals for the Tier 1 study.

Project Website: http://www.newbergdundeebypass.org/

Placer and Sutter County ROW Preservation

Project Summary

The Placer Parkway is an approximately 15-mile long, 4-6 lane, high-speed roadway transportation facility with up to six interchanges, connecting SR 65 to SR 70/99. It will link existing and planned development near some of the region's fastest growing communities while improving access to the I-5 corridor, downtown Sacramento, and the Sacramento International Airport. The project is to preserve ROW in this rapidly developing area to respond to existing / anticipated travel demand and congestion and to provide access to the regional transportation system for jobs growth. The corridor currently being examined extends from 500-feet to 1000-feet in width.   .

Tiering Process

The NOI to develop a Tier 1 EIS was published on September 18, 2003 with the Tier 1 DEIS being released on July 2, 2007. The Tier 1 FEIS is anticipated to be released in the summer of 2009. The tiered process is being used to identify a corridor and preserve ROW along the approximately 15-miles long, 500 to 1,000 feet wide corridor. The Tier 1 analyzed over 50 alternatives considering various modes and corridor variations. Tier 1 put forth five alternatives with an additional four variations based upon these alternatives each.

Highlights

- The process was defined through a modified NEPA/404 agreement. This was later interpreted differently by the resource agencies and other parties, leading to a discrepancy over the level of detail appropriate to a Tier 1 environmental document.

- There was a perception on this project that the early and continuous involvement of the resource agencies and early identification of the concurrence points would have helped to streamline the process without negatively affecting Tier 2.

- A major issue that is impacting this project is the development of the Placer County Habitat Conservation Plan which will establish "reserve areas" where the county will focus its land preservation efforts. It is estimated that agreement upon this plan will not be until around 2010 and therefore the resource agencies seem reluctant to commit to a corridor until it is determined where the reserve areas will be located. Additionally, once this plan is in place, it is anticipated that efforts to identify a corridor and an alignment will be much easier.

- An MOU was developed between the Placer County Transportation Planning Agency (PCTPA), FHWA, Caltrans, and the federal resource agencies – U.S. ACOE and the U.S. EPA on the NEPA/404 process which outlines the agreement to identify environmental issues that could affect future construction permit approvals.

Project Website: http://www.pctpa.org/placerparkway/index.htm

Richmond to Hampton Roads

Project Summary

The project is to improve passenger rail service between Richmond Virginia, and Hampton Roads in the Norfolk area, and to ultimately be an extension of the Southeast High Speed Rail Corridor. Various speed trains were examined for alignments on both the north and south sides of the James River.

Tiering Process

The NOI to develop a Tier 1 EIS for this project was published on February 23, 2004, and the Tier 1 DEIS is still being developed by the Virginia Department of Rail and Public Transportation (DRPT) along with the FRA. The tiering approach was adopted because of the length of the project (100 miles if the north alternative is chosen, 140 miles if the southern route is chosen) and because of the complexity of the project which was considering various high speed rail options and routes which ran partially or completely on both the north and south sides of the James River.

Highlights

- High staff turnover at the agencies as well as at the DOT and FRA has led to a changing of the project's goals and objectives, including the request to consider a new alternative which would have caused a change in the NOI, P&N, etc....

- The tiered process allowed the project to examine more options with less detail and therefore more quickly and less expensively.

- The parties interviewed for this project felt there should be more guidance, regulations, and standards, detailing what should be included within each Tier of a Tiered document.

- The general opinion was that as pieces of the document are developed, these sections should be signed off on providing an administrative record so that when the administrative draft is released the project team is aware of what is being submitted.

- The project has to balance competing interests from the north and south sides of the river as the majority of rail development has been on the north side of the river. Again the north side is showing fewer environmental impacts, fewer freight conflicts, a better cost effectiveness, and similar ridership with only slightly less ridership than a route combining both the north and south sides.

- An MOU was developed with the SHPO for the Tier 1 process with the understanding that the SHPO will be able to have additional input during Tier 2.

- Two previous studies of passenger rail service improvements for this area have been conducted. One Major Investment Study (MIS) in 1999 and a feasibility study in 2002.

- This project is part of the Southeast High Speed Rail Corridor.

Project Website: http://www.rich2hrrail.info/index.html

South Florida East Coast Corridor

Project Summary

The Florida DOT is leading a regional partnership with the FTA to conduct the South Florida East Coast Corridor (SFECC) Transit Analysis Study. The study purpose is to develop and analyze alternatives that potentially integrate passenger and freight transport along the SFECC. This study is being done in an effort to relieve roadway congestion while providing needed freight transport to the area. The corridor is 85 miles long and two miles wide. Existing commuter services are in the study area, and a principal alignment is an existing active freight railroad corridor.

Tiering Process

The NOI to conduct a Tier 1 study was published on March 28, 2006. A Draft Tier 1 Programmatic EIS (PEIS) was prepared, and several versions of the Final PEIS were prepared. SFECC will continue to complete advanced alternatives analysis under an Early Scoping Notice. This will allow for advancing Tier 1 decisions into Tier 2. When final mode and alignment are determined, the Tier 1 FEIS will be completed and a ROD will be issued.

Highlights

- The FTA felt that a final mode and general alignment should have been decided at the conclusion of Tier 1 while the state DOT preferred to identify various modes at different points in the corridor and only identified a corridor and not a specific alignment at the end of the Tier 1 process. The FTA felt there was no proposed action on which they could issue a ROD.

- An FTA concern was that the state DOT did not follow the FTA's project development process. FTA preferred that the Alternatives Analysis be complete and an individual mode and alignment selected with the issuance of a Tier 1 ROD.

- The state DOT's concerns were that FTA had not conducted a Tiered EIS process due to staff turnover between the initiation of the project and the review of the Tier 1 documentation.

- Another difficultly identified during the project interviews was coordinating with many of the resource agencies who either did not want to be involved until permitting was necessary, or wanted traditional NEPA analysis performed on each of the over 20 Tier 1 alternatives.

- Keys to success would be the involvement of the resource agencies, early and often in the process and utilizing an MOU or MOA to document the decision to follow the process and the objectives.

Project Website: http://www.sfeccstudy.com/

Southeast High Speed Rail

Project Summary

The Southeast High Speed Rail project involves the development of high speed rail service along the 500-mile corridor from Washington, D.C. to Charlotte, North Carolina along existing rail rights-of-way. The Rail Division of the North Carolina Department of Transportation (NCDOT) is leading the project development in coordination with the Virginia Department of Rail and Public Transportation (VDRPT). FHWA and the Federal Rail Administration (FRA) are lead federal agencies for NEPA. Potential project effects include impacts on the human environment, impacts to historic properties, and impacts to wetlands and floodplains. The state agencies are currently conducting the Tier 2 study.

Tiering Process

Tiering was selected for the project because of the geographic scale of the project and because of the numerous alternative study areas and existing rail rights-of-way. NCDOT, in cooperation with VDRPT and the federal agencies, began the Tier 1 study upon publication of the Notice of Intent on August 5, 1999. A Record of Decision for the Tier 1 EIS was published in October 2002. The Tier 1 EIS examined corridor alternatives for the rail project and identified a 6-mile wide preferred corridor centered on existing rail rights-of-way. Although the Tier 1 ROD did not identify the termini for the Tier 2 sections, the Tier 2 termini were proposed in a separate document, a Draft Implementation Plan, issued in the same month as the Tier 1 ROD. Some efforts were taken in Tier 1 to comply with non-NEPA review requirements. In Tier 2, the agencies are conducting separate engineering and environmental studies for each section. A Tier 2 EIS for the Richmond to Raleigh section began in 2003 and is expected to be completed by the end of 2011. Categorical exclusions are being prepared for many actions outside the Richmond to Raleigh portion of the corridor.

Highlights

- Early in the project's development, FHWA, FRA, NCDOT, and VDRPT entered into a Memorandum of Understanding to coordinate and document each agency's respective roles and responsibilities in conducting the environmental studies.

- Shortly after the tiered process began, the project team developed a scoping process to gather input from federal and state agencies and the public. The scoping process involved informal communications with resource agencies, a formal joint bi-state scoping meeting, formation of an advisory committee, and other public involvement activities.

- The project team engaged in extensive public involvement activities, including conducting surveys of approximately 7,000 individuals, holding public workshops and public hearings, and sending direct mailings. The agencies also held media briefings.

- Some difficulties were encountered with respect to interstate coordination as a result of the differing priorities of the two states and differences in funding sources.

Project Website: http://www.sehsr.org/

Trans Texas Corridor – 35 (TTC-35)

Project Summary

The proposed TTC-35 is approximately 600 miles long, extending from Dallas/Fort Worth to Mexico and possibly on to the Gulf Coast. TTC-35 parallels the existing I-35. The study area is approximately four to ten miles wide, bulging to 18 miles wide. TTC-35 would include separate lanes for passenger vehicles and large trucks, freight railways, high speed commuter railways, and a corridor for utilities including water lines, oil and natural gas pipelines, and transmission lines for electricity, broadband and other telecommunication services.

Tiering Process

The tiered approach was adopted by the Texas Department of Transportation (TxDOT) at the initiation of the project. The geographic scale of the project, the time needed to complete the project (30-70 years) and overall project size were all major considerations in deciding to use tiering. Tiering was chosen initially for corridor preservation, particularly in areas where land was rapidly developing, but this was prevented through actions by the Texas legislature.

Highlights

- No partnership agreements or partnering manuals were developed for the project, but the agencies and metropolitan planning organizations were involved early and often in project development.

- The lead agencies did not encounter any major issues with the resource agencies.

- Staff turnover at resource agencies caused delays on the project

- The greatest identified weakness of the process was a lack of understanding about the tiered process on behalf of the public.

- The biggest issue cited was pre-planning, engaging local officials early on, and putting together focus groups so the public could understand what they were trying to accomplish by using the tiered process.

Project Website: http://ttc.keeptexasmoving.com/projects/ttc35/

U.S. 50, Colorado

Project Summary

The project proposes transportation improvements on US highway 50 between Pueblo, Colorado and the vicinity of the Kansas State line in southeastern Colorado. The corridor is approximately 150 miles long and four miles wide, connecting four counties and 10 municipalities. The project began as a corridor study along the western portion of the corridor, but there arose a sense that the corridor was used by all of the communities along the 150 miles to access Pueblo. These communities stressed that the entire 150 miles needed studied and that the project as proposed is needed as US 50 currently functions as the main street in the 10 communities through the corridor. Because of this a new alignment around the towns are being identified to increase safety and mobility throughout the corridor.

Tiering Process

The NOI to conduct a Tier 1 study was published on January 30, 2006. The tiered process was chosen to consider the entire corridor at once as improvements to one section would not have resulted in significant safety or travel time improvements. Additionally, it was hoped that by completing the initial NEPA study, the US 50 corridor would be positioned to solicit funds from the state for Tier 2. The project team, headed by the Colorado DOT in cooperation with the FHWA is currently writing the Tier 1 DEIS. In Tier 1, the team will identify a mode choice and a preferred 1,000 foot wide corridor. To date (October 2008), it has been determined that the mode will be only highway and that US 50 will be developed as a divided 4-land highway mostly on the current alignment with bypasses around the towns. Currently there is no funding to build this project or to initiate the Tier 2 NEPA process. The team will be working with local communities to preserve ROW, but there is no money available to purchase ROW at this time. ROW cannot be purchased until the Tier 2 document is completed.

Highlights

- A major study for the possible improvements to US 50 from Pueblo to Kansas was completed prior to starting the Tiered project.

- Pre-scoping meetings for the tiered document with the agencies was a factor contributing to the success of this project. It developed trust and raised major issues while all of the parties were at the table which otherwise would not have been uncovered until later.

- Developed a work plan at the beginning of the project to identify goals, risks, and to set expectations among the agencies. Presented resource methodologies during the scoping meetings. This was viewed a major reason for the success of the project to date.

- An agency charter and a community charter were developed, identifying what information would be provided, when it would be provided, and when input from the agencies and the communities would be requested.

Project Website: http://www.dot.state.co.us/US50E/

U.S. 301, Maryland

Project Summary

The project was originally proposed in 1993 to examine US 301. In 1995 the Maryland State Highway Administration (MSHA) was directed to transition these recommendations into the NEPA process. The project involves improvements along an existing 50 mile corridor of U.S. 301 due to projected population growth and development. The project was broken into two sections with independent utility, with each following the tiered process. The 20 mile northern section extends along US 301 from the US 301/MD5 interchange at T.B. to US 50. The 39 mile southern section extends from the Governor Nice Bridge to the 301/MD5 interchange at T.B. (30 miles), and along the MD5 corridor from T.B. to the Capital Beltway (I-95/I-495) (9 miles). The Tier 1 work would focus on the approval of purpose and need, mode, and corridors to allow the use of federal funding for protective ROW purchases. Subsequent "break-out" projects under Tier 2 would follow a more traditional NEPA approach for specific location/design approval.

The Tier 1 DEIS for the northern section was completed in 1998 and a ROD issued in 2001. Work in the southern section began in 1998 with the intention of doing a Tier 1 document for the entire section while concurrently developing a Tier 2 document for the northern portion in the Waldorf area. The entire project was put on hold in 2001.

In 2005 it was determined that the southern section around the Waldorf area and the 9-mile section of MD5 extending to I-95/I-495 would no longer follow the tiered process and would instead follow a traditional EIS process. This was due to rapid growth and the need to quickly make improvements to this area. Improvements to other more southern sections such as La Plata were not seen as critical, and their short-term transportation needs on US 301 would be addressed as part of an access management plan.

Tiering Process

The FHWA in cooperation with the MSHA and the ACOE published a NOI to prepare a combined Tier 1/Tier 2 EIS for the southern most 39 miles of the project (MD5 and La Plata corridors) in April 12, 2000. This section is currently developing the DEIS. The tiering process was adopted because of the project length and lack of available funding to conduct a traditional study for the entire 50 miles. Currently (October 2008) one of the sections of independent utility identified in the northern section, Maryland 197 from Mount Hope Road to US 50., is in Tier 2.

Highlights

- Involvement and commitment from the senior management at the resource agencies is important to facilitating the project early on.

- An environmental methodology matrix was developed to coordinate with the agencies on the level of detail that would be conducted in Tier 1 and Tier 2.

- Programmatic agreement with SHPO, to carry forward to Tier 2, information from Tier 1.

- Maryland corridor preservation may be done through a county's long range plan and therefore a ROD on a Tiered EIS is only necessary for corridor preservation if federal funds are needed to preserve the ROW.

Project Website: http://www.us301waldorf.org/pages/project/planschedule.htm

Winchester-Temecula Corridor – Riverside California

Project Summary

      The project consisted of adding 4-6 lanes, over 10 miles along I-15 and I-215 between Temecula and Newport Rd near Winchester. The initial project analyzed a new corridor, but a hybrid alternative which assumed widening of the existing interstates received approval in the ROD. The decision through Tier 1 has been made to widen the existing interstate with a new lane in each direction, added in the median. Current funding only allows for adding one lane in each direction. The hope is to add additional lanes at a later date, but current funding only allows for the current addition of one lane in each direction.

Tiering Process

      The NOI to conduct a Tier 1 EIS study for this corridor was published on August 2, 2001. Tiering was adopted to preserve ROW throughout the corridor at a width of about 500 ft as funding for construction was not available. The Tier 1 ROD was received in September 2003 and allowed for the preservation of the ROW and set forth alternatives for the potential addition of lanes outside of the median at a later date, however, the project team is currently dependent upon local cities to preserve the ROW by placing conditions against development in these areas. The Tier 1 EIS was primarily developed by the Riverside County Transportation Commission (RCTC) in conjunction with the FHWA, California DOT, and the County of Riverside.

Highlights

- The development of guidelines on the level of detail required would have been very helpful as the project team was constantly asked to gather more detailed data.

- A meeting early on in the process to get all of the parties to agree on what the goal of Tier 1 was would have been very helpful.

- A partnership agreement with the agencies was developed to conduct conservation planning to preserve 153,000 acres in the vicinity of the project, but the acquisition of this property has not been completed which has delayed agency approval of the project.

- The project team felt that millions of dollars and much time could have been saved by conducting a corridor study, and the team does not feel they are any further ahead by conducting a tiered EIS.

Project Website: www.rcip.org / http://www.rcip.org/wt_toc.htm

Wisconsin U.S. 10

Project Summary

The initial Tier 1 US 10 project covered approximately 60 miles from Waupaca to Marshfield upgrading the highway from a 2-lane rural highway to a 4-lane expressway with much of these upgrades being on existing alignment with some new alignment utilized to avoid development. The Wisconsin DOT was responsible for developing the environmental documentation in cooperation with the FHWA. The Eastern Portion from County Highway J (CTH-J) east of Stevens Point to Waupaca was done as a more detailed analysis and the project moved directly into construction after receiving the ROD. The remainder of the corridor analysis was done for corridor preservation as there is substantial development anticipated to occur in the vicinity of the corridor.

Tiering Process

The decision to follow the tiered EIS process for US 10 in Wisconsin was made in the early 1990's with the Tier 1 FEIS for the entire 60 mile section from Marshfield to Waupaca being approved in 2000. While this Tier 1 was being undertaken, a traditional EIS was simultaneously being conducted for the section along the eastern section of the corridor from Amherst Junction to Waupaca. The project was initially viewed in three sections, but because decisions made in one section would have affected the other sections, the decision was made to utilize tiering.

In Tier 1 sections of independent utility were identified for Tier 2 analysis. These sections were from County Highway J (CTH-J) east of Stevens Point to Waupaca (construction completed), from Junction City to Stevens Point (under construction), from Marshfield to Junction City (currently under design), and from Stevens Point to Amherst Junction (currently under design / environmental evaluation). This last section out to Amherst Junction is being completed to allow for corridor preservation by the state. Construction in this section is not expected until 2025.

The NOI to conduct a Tier 2 EIS to improve US 10 in Wisconsin from Junction City to Stevens Point was published in September 7, 2001.

Highlights

- The consensus was that the process was likely made more difficult by combining Tier 1 and Tier 2 processes for the eastern section because some of the other sections of independent utility when moved forward into Tier 2 had to be reevaluated which affected the completed section of CTH-J east of Stevens Point to Waupaca.

- The public was concerned and confused about the process and the land being identified for ROW. They also felt the Tier 1 did not provide enough detail

- The tiering process eliminated concerns about logical termini and helped to guide development.

Project Website:　http://www.dot.state.wi.us/projects/us10/index.htm